Political Agendas for Education

From the Religious Right to the Green Party

Second Edition

Sociocultural, Political, and Historical Studies in Education

Joel Spring, Editor

Political Agendas for Education

From the Religious Right to the Green Party

Second Edition

Joel Spring
New School University

LEA LAWRENCE ERLBAUM ASSOCIATES, PUBLISHERS
2002 Mahwah, New Jersey   London

Lawrence Erlbaum Associates, Inc., Publishers
10 Industrial Avenue
Mahwah, NJ 07430

Cover design by Kathryn Houghtaling Lacey

Library of Congress Cataloging-in-Publication Data

Spring, Joel H.
Political agendas for education : from the religious right to the Green Party /
  Joel Spring. — 2nd ed.
    p.   cm.
Includes bibliographical references and index.
ISBN 0-8058-3984-4 (cloth : alk. paper) — ISBN 0-8058-3985-2 (pbk. : alk. paper)
  1. Politics and education—United States.   2. Liberalism—United States.
3. Conservatism—United States.   I. Title.
LC89.S663   2002
379.73—dc21

                                                        2001040927
                                                            CIP

Books published by Lawrence Erlbaum Associates are printed on acid-free paper,
and their bindings are chosen for strength and durability.

Printed in the United States of America
10 9 8 7 6 5 4 3 2 1

Contents

◆ ◆ ◆

Preface

Pick up any newspaper today and you will find some political group demanding the censorship of school materials or the inclusion in schools of their pet ideas, or they will be proposing another quick fix for educational ills or making claims that their educational plans will be panaceas for all economic and social problems. Educational disputes range across a political spectrum, from the agendas of the crusading religious right to the separatist feelings of Afrocentrists and Indiocentrists.

My goal in this book is to describe and analyze the educational agendas of major political organizations. I begin with the outrage of evangelical parents at what they perceive to be the anti-Christian curricula of public schools. At the other end of the political spectrum covered in this book is the Green party which, under the leadership of Ralph Nader in the 2000 Presidential election, attacked the growing commercialization of public schools and demanded protection for children from the consumerist ideology of advertising.

In this second edition I describe the changes in political agendas for education that occurred during the 2000 Presidential election. Of major importance was the election of President George W. Bush, whose ideology reflects writings on compassionate conservativeness and the work of the Manhattan Institute, a conservative think tank. The selection of Ralph Nader to lead the Green party brought into prominence an explicit attack on the ideology of consumerism. New topics in the second edition are:

- The Republican educational agenda for the 21st century

- The meaning of "compassionate conservative"
- Evolution versus creationism
- The Manhattan Institute and George W. Bush's educational policies
- Gore and the 2000 Presidential campaign
- What's left of the left? Ralph Nader and the Green party
- Ralph Nader, consumerism, and education

Chapter 1

Compassionate Conservatives: The Republican Educational Agenda for the 21st Century

◆ ◆ ◆

After waking up with a hangover from his 40th birthday party at Colorado's posh Broadmoor Hotel, George W. Bush vowed to give up alcohol and focus on Bible studies. Rejecting his former dissipated life, the future President began to hangout with a Fort Worth televangelist named James Robison, who claimed to regularly chat with God while driving on the freeway between Dallas and Arlington, Texas. Bush's attachment to the religious right would eventually lead him down the thorny path of educational politics as governor of Texas and President of the United States. His sincere religious commitment would also provide him with the self-proclaimed title of "Compassionate Conservative."[1]

While George W. Bush was undergoing his religious revelations, his future Secretary of Education Rod Paige was beginning his transition from football coach to educational leader. In 1969 at Indiana University, Paige earned his PhD in physical education with a 123-page dissertation titled "The Effect of Pre-Foreperiod Preparation and Foreperiod Duration Upon the Response Time of Football Lineman." The study determined the best conditions for getting fast starts from football linemen, and it concluded with a recommendation for further study of "the response time of football linemen for lateral movements."[2] Paige's leadership skills were evident as he quickly rose through the coaching ranks to become head football coach at Texas Southern University in the 1970s and eventually dean of the school's College of Education between 1984 and 1990. From there it was a quick step to the superintendency of the Houston school district in 1994, where his managerial skills caught the attention of then-Governor Bush. After Bush selected Paige in 2001 to be Secretary of Education, George Chaump, the head coach of the Central Dauphin High School Rams in Harrisburg, Pennsylvania, commented about the appointment, "I don't think you could be a good coach unless you're a great teacher first. If he's been on the football field and in the classroom, he's well qualified to be secretary."[3]

What linked the compassionate conservative Bush to the football coach Paige was their fervent belief in the ability of state-mandated testing and phonics-based reading drills to give every child a chance to succeed in America. As superintendent of the Houston schools, Paige oversaw a skill-and-drill curriculum geared to preparing students for Texas-mandated statewide tests. Calling her story "Drilling in Texas," Kathleen Manzo wrote about the Houston reading program, "Teachers in Houston are marching in lockstep to fulfill district orders that basic skills make up the core of their reading curriculum." She described the following scene in a Houston kindergarten:

> The children sit in neat rows on the floor, their legs crisscrossed, hands in their laps. In unison, they sound out the letters, their voices loud and clear, as part of the morning reading drill. In the singsong tones of a military cadence, they work their way through the alphabet:
> "A, a, what do you say, ah, ah, ah ... ," they chant.
> "B, b, what do you say, buh, buh, buh ... "[4]

Statewide testing is another side of educational drills. Similar to football, Paige argued, education must maintain a scoreboard in its end zone. Speaking to the American Council of Education on February 20, 2001, Paige drew the following parallel between football and schooling: "To make sure that our schools are really teaching children, we ask the states to measure the results. You know, I'm an old football coach, so it just makes sense to me that if you want to win the football game you have to first keep score. That big scoreboard in the end zone tells you whether you are ahead or behind and how long you've got left to try to win the game."[5]

Avoiding the issues surrounding the effect of testing on standardization of knowledge and forcing teachers to teach from a script geared to the test, Paige criticized, "Those who argue against testing our children essentially argue that we shouldn't put that scoreboard up there, that we shouldn't worry about winning the battle for literacy or losing it, and that we shouldn't worry about how long that child has left before he's so far behind that he can't catch up."[6]

THE MEANING OF "COMPASSIONATE CONSERVATIVE"

George W. Bush's self-proclaimed title of "compassionate conservative" was derived from the work of University of Texas journalism professor Marvin Olasky. In his office on the Austin campus, located only a short distance from the Texas state capitol building, Olasky professed the need for a rebirth of American compassion. As editor of the weekly news-magazine *Christian* and as author of two important books, *The Tragedy of American Compassion* and *Renewing American Compassion*, Olasky blamed government welfare programs for worsening the moral conditions of the poor and, as a result, perpetuating poverty in the United States. Olasky's answer to helping the poor was returning welfare programs to faith-based organizations.

Influenced by Olasky's *Renewing American Compassion*, Bush proposed during his 2000 campaign and later as President that faith-based organization should be allowed to compete for federal funds. Regarding education, Bush proposed funding after-school activities operated by faith-based organization. In reference to federal after-school programs of the 21st Century Community Learning Centers program originally created during the Clinton years, Bush suggested "introduc[ing] legislation to open 100 percent of the 21st Century programs funding to competitive bidding ... [to] allow youth development groups, local charities, churches, synagogues, mosques and other community and faith-based organizations to compete for these federal funds on an equal footing with schools."[7]

Federal programs operated by faith-based groups, according to Olasky and other compassionate conservatives, would ensure the teaching of traditional moral values to America's poor. To Olasky, humans are basically sinful, and their inherent sinfulness must be curbed by moral instruction. The danger of providing welfare funds without demanding work in return, he argues, is that humans can easily slip into a depraved condition. Olasky maintained that in "orthodox Christian anthropology . . . man's sinful nature leads toward indolence, and that an impoverished person given a dole without obligation is likely to descend into pauperism."[8]

Reforming the government welfare system is fruitless, according to Olasky, because constitutional restrictions do not allow bureaucrats to teach religious values. The only hope, he argues, is to replace government programs with charities operated by faith-based organizations. Olasky supports his argument with a historical survey of private charities that includes the exhortation of 17th-century Puritan divine Cotton Mather: "Don't nourish [the idle] and harden'em in that, but find employment for them. Find'em work; set'em to work; keep'em to work."[9]

Olasky maintains that there are beneficial results from a direct relationship between the giver and receiver as opposed to a the relationship
between a faceless government bureaucracy and the receiver. Giving, he
declares, is a moral act. Personal charity provides benefits to the giver
through engagement with the suffering of others. The engagement with
suffering supposedly strengthens the religious faith of the giver which, in
turn, results in providing a model of religious values for the recipient.
Consequently, replacing government-operated welfare programs with
faith-based and personal charity, according to Olasky, strengthens the
general moral values of society while providing the poor with a real
means of escaping poverty. Regarding the Christian definition of compassion, Olasky stated that "The word points to personal involvement with
the needy, suffering with them, not just giving to them. 'Suffering with'
means adopting hard-to-place babies, providing shelter to women undergoing crisis . . . working one-on-one with a single mother."[10]

In a strange twist, Olasky is able to link the concept of compassionate
conservative to Bush's 2001 tax cut proposal. In reference to what he
calls "compassion fatigue," Olasky argued that, "Many Americans who
would like to contribute more of their money and time are weighed down
by tax burdens."[11] This suggests an interesting scenario of a tax cut allowing more time and money for personal charity, which in turn would result
in a moral reformation of the nation.

TEACHING VALUES VERSUS CHANGING THE ECONOMIC SYSTEM

The compassionate conservative's emphasis on teaching moral values is
proclaimed in another book that influenced Bush. As Governor of Texas,
Bush wrote that

> Dream and the Nightmare by Myron Magnet crystallized for me the impact
> the failed culture of the sixties had on our values and society. It helped
> create dependency on government, undermine family and eroded values
> which had stood the test of time and which are critical if we want a decent
> and hopeful tomorrow for every single American.[12]

Editor of the ultraconservative Manhattan Institute's City Journal and
former member of the editorial board of Fortune magazine, Myron Magnet considers the 1960s and early 1970s the cultural watershed of American history. During this period American values, he argued, deteriorated
as a result of a cultural revolution led "by an elite of opinion makers,
policymakers, and mythmakers—lawyers, judges, professors, political

staffers, journalists, writers, TV and movie honchos, clergymen—and it was overwhelmingly a liberal, left-of-center elite."[13] Out of this cultural revolution, according to Magnet, emerged a whole host of programs, including the War on Poverty, court-ordered busing, affirmative action, drug treatment programs, and the political correctness movement at colleges.

Most important, Magnet argues, the cultural revolution overturned the traditional American values that supported hard work and family life as the basis for economic success and good living. The new values were represented by two "epochal" expressions. The first was the sexual revolution, which Magnet feels resulted in increased divorce, illegitimacy, and female-headed families. The second was the 1960s counterculture that rejected an unjust economic system and hard work.

Basic to Magnet's argument is a belief that values determine the economic and social systems as compared to the assumption that the social and economic systems determine values. In other words, similar to Olasky, Magnet believes that the major liberal error was to try to eliminate poverty by changing the economic system as opposed to changing the values of the poor. Magnet presented the following argument:

> On the grandest level, if you believe that human choices and actions, rather than blind, impersonal forces, determine the shape of history, then the ideas and visions impelling the human actors become crucial causes of the reality that unfolds. Men don't simply have their environment handed to them from on high; they collectively make and remake it from the cultural and material resources that lie ready at hand. And great men augment those resources by inventing new techniques and new ideas.[14]

Within this framework of thinking Magnet argues that American society advanced because of the Protestant values that promoted a free economy. Citing Max Weber, Magnet identifies these values as individualism, hard work, and a belief that success is a sign of God's blessing.

Other conservatives echo Magnet's sentiments. Pat Buchanan, the conservative political commentator and 2000 presidential candidate for the Reform Party, provided the following description of the beliefs of the religious right: "Among the social conservatives [of the Republican Party] resides the Religious Right to whom the expulsion of God from the classroom, the rise of the drug culture, and the 'sexual revolution' are unmistakable symptoms of cultural decadence and national decline."[15]

In contrast, Michael Lind, a former conservative and at present a critic of the right, argued that right-wing Republicans, such as Buchanan and Olasky, launched a cultural war against public schools as a method of diverting "the wrath of wage-earning populist voters from Wall Street and corporate America to other targets: the universities, the media, racial minorities, homosexuals, immigrants."[16] In fact, Lind referred to conservative claims of a crisis in public education as their "second great policy hoax," which resulted in many Americans being persuaded that the schools are failing the nation.[17]

Although criticism of public schools, as Lind suggested, might be a distraction from the growing economic inequalities in U.S. society, no one who has sat through school board meetings or read court transcripts involving debates over sex education, school prayer, secular humanism, censorship of textbooks, and school choice can doubt the strong beliefs of the Republican right. Drawing its support from well-organized evangelical Christians, the religious right has launched a crusade to save American education and democracy.

MORALITY AND DEMOCRACY

The desire by the religious right to gain control of schools and the media is based on a belief that ideas determine social conditions. Buchanan quoted Mazzini: "Ideas rule the world and its events. A revolution is a passage of an idea from theory to practice. Whatever men say, material interests never caused and never will cause a revolution."[18] Agreeing with Buchanan, William Bennett, who served 9 years in public office as head of the National Endowment for the Humanities, as Secretary of Education under Ronald Reagan, and as drug czar under George Bush, stated that "I have come to the conclusion that the issues surrounding the culture and our values are the most important ones …. They are at the heart of our resolution of the knottiest problems of public policy, whether the subject be education, art, race relations, drugs, crime, or raising children."[19] For Bennett, the solution to public problems was teaching of morality and Western cultural values.

The religious right believes that a well-functioning democracy depends on the morality of the individual. This particular belief was prevalent among U.S. leaders during the period after the American Revolution. Revolutionary leaders believed in a concept of Christian liberty in which true freedom required a belief in God. Within this context a democratic polity can safely function only when all citizens are controlled by their belief in a common morality and culture. From this perspective, the role of public schools in a democracy is to instill Christian morality and a common culture.[20]

To support the conviction that an acceptance of Christ and Christian morality are necessary for maintaining democracy, William Bennett quoted George Washington's farewell address: "Of all the dispositions and habits which lead to political prosperity, religion and morality are indispensable supports .... And let us with caution indulge the supposition that morality can be maintained without religion."[21]

With similar language, Ralph Reed, a founder of the Christian Coalition and its first executive director, argued that democracy depends on citizens and their government showing allegiance to God. "In this greater moral context," Reed stated, "faith as a political force is not undemocratic; it is the very essence of democracy."[22]

Believing in the overriding importance of Christian morality and culture for solving social problems and maintaining democracy, the religious right supports school prayer, school choice, abolition of secular humanism in public schools, censorship of textbooks and books in school libraries, restricting sex education to teaching abstinence, and stopping the spread of multiculturalism.

THE REPUBLICAN PARTY AND THE CHRISTIAN COALITION

Currently, the Christian Coalition is the largest political organization representing the religious right. The Christian Coalition was organized in 1989 by televangelist Pat Robertson and Ralph Reed after Pat Robertson's unsuccessful Presidential campaign in 1988. In 2001, the organization claimed an membership of more than 1.5 million, working in 1,500 chapters in all 50 states, with central headquarters located in Washington, DC. Robertson described the group as "a coalition of pro-family Roman Catholics, evangelicals, and other people of faith working together to become the unified voice of families with children in middle class America."[23]

The religious right became affiliated with the Republican Party because of shifting patterns of political allegiances. In the 1970s and 1980s, Republican leaders tried to break the attachment of southern Whites and northern White ethnic groups to the Democratic Party. During the early 1970s, President Richard Nixon consciously supported affirmative action policies as a method of dividing the Democratic coalition of northern White union members, White ethnic groups, and minority groups. In part, the Democrats contributed to their losses by supporting affirmative-action hiring as opposed to race-neutral hiring. This resulted in a major realignment of parties, with many northern urban Whites flocking to the Republican camp.[24]

Also, Nixon hoped to win over traditional southern White Democrats by opposing the integration of schools by the busing of students. The traditional Democratic southern power structure was built around racist policies, including the segregation of public schools. Many Whites were alienated from the national Democratic Party because of its support of civil rights and therefore joined the Republican Party. In addition, many southern Blacks, who had traditionally viewed the Republican Party as the party of Lincoln, joined the Democratic party.

Underlying these racial politics were religious politics. This combination of racial and religious politics had a profound effect on Republican policies regarding schools. After U.S. Supreme Court rulings in the 1960s prohibiting officially conducted school prayers and Bible reading, many evangelical Christians declared the public school system an enemy of Christianity and began sending their children to newly created private Christian academies. Fears of racial integration and godless classrooms resulted in the rapid growth of private Christian schools. Like Catholic parents, who thought it unfair to be taxed for support of public schools while they were paying tuition for religious schools, evangelicals demanded government support of private schools. Initiating a "school choice" movement, evangelicals argued that state and federal governments should provide financial assistance so that parents could make a choice for their children between public and private schools.[25]

Reed claimed that evangelical Christians abandoned the Democratic Party in the late 1970s when the head of the Internal Revenue Service in the Carter administration required Christian schools to prove that they were not established to preserve segregation. During the early 1970s there were rumblings that many of the Christian academies in the South were created as havens for White students fleeing integration. In Reed's words, "More than any other single episode, the IRS move against Christian schools sparked the explosion of the movement that would become known as the religious right."[26]

The use of religious politics by the Republican Party is exemplified by a 1996 interview with James Pinkerton, an advisor to the Reagan and Bush administrations and author of *What Comes Next: The End of Big Government—And the New Paradigm Ahead*. In response to a question about divisions within the Republican Party, Pinkerton replied:

> Thirty years ago, Kevin Phillips, Pat Buchanan, and people like that were strategizing that we, the Republicans, win over all the southern Fundamentalists and all northern urban Catholics, and we'll build a new American majority party. And that sort of has happened. We won over a lot of urban Catholics and the South is now Republican."[27]

Responding to the same question, William Kristol, former chief of staff to Dan Quayle and editor of the *Weekly Standard*, said that "The Republicans made the right bet demographically to bet against Episcopalians, Methodists, and Presbyterians, and with Evangelicals."[28]

The result of what has been called the "southernization" of the Republican Party was a split between Republicans who were primarily interested in issues regarding abortion, morality, culture, and schools and those who were primarily interested in economic issues. From the perspective of the religious right, moderate Republicans were concerned with protecting the interests of big business. Reed wanted the Republican Party to become "the party of Main Street, not Wall Street." He went on to claim that "the real battle for the soul of our nation is not fought primarily over the gross national product and the prime interest rate, but over virtues, values, and the culture."[29] Echoing Reed, Buchanan rejected moderate Republican ties to business and, parodying Calvin Coolidge, said, "The business of America is not business."[30]

One leader of the so-called "electronic church," Jerry Falwell, took the concerns of the religious right directly to the 1980 Republican presidential candidate, Ronald Reagan. Falwell's television program, Old-Time Gospel Hour, was seen in more than 12 million homes in the United States. In 1979, before meeting with Reagan, Falwell attended a lunch sponsored by the Heritage Foundation. Its director, Paul Weyrich, told him there was a "moral majority" waiting for a call to political action. Falwell jumped at the phrase and named his group the Moral Majority. Under Falwell's leadership, the organization held rallies around the country supporting the legalization of school prayer, school choice, and abolition of abortion. Within a space of 2 years, the Moral Majority had 2 million members and was raising $10 million annually.[31]

The wedding between Ronald Reagan and the Moral Majority occurred shortly after the 1980 Republican convention when Reagan was asked to address 20,000 evangelicals at a rally in Dallas. Reagan told the group, "I know that you cannot endorse me [because of the tax-exempt status of the Moral Majority], but I endorse you and everything you do."[32] Giving hope to evangelicals opposed to evolutionary theory, Reagan expressed doubts about the plausibility of Darwinian ideas. After the 1980 election, Reagan supported the religious right's agenda by endorsing legislation for a tuition tax credit to allow parents to choose between public and private schools and by promising to support a school prayer amendment. After 1980, school choice and school prayer became a standard fixture in Republican platforms.

By 1996, the political power of evangelical Christians working through the Christian Coalition was a fixture in Republican politics. For instance,

Presidential candidate Bob Dole wanted to focus on an economic agenda while avoiding a strong stand against abortion, but the Christian Coalition threatened to disrupt the 1996 convention unless the party platform opposed abortion. Consequently, the committee writing the Republican platform capitulated to the religious right by including the following plank in the 1996 Republican Party Platform: "The unborn has a fundamental individual right to life which cannot be infringed. We support a human life amendment to the Constitution and we endorse legislation to make clear that the Fourteenth Amendment's protections apply to unborn children."[33]

One news release about the abortion plank stated that it "was dramatic evidence of what analysts have been saying for the last few years: that religious conservatives, mainly White evangelical Protestants, have established a dominant position in the Republican Party machinery under the umbrella of the Christian Coalition."[34] Susan Cullman, chairwoman of the Republican Coalition for Choice, said in disgust, "It looks like [Dole is] being led by the religious right."[35]

Whereas press coverage was given to the religious right's influence on the abortion plank in the 1996 Republican platform, little attention was given to its influence on the education plank that supported the religious right's agenda, including opposition to education about birth control, support of abstinence education, abolition of the federal Department of Education, support of voluntary school prayer, opposition to multiculturalism, and support of a patriotic and Western civilization-oriented curriculum.[36] The education plank opened with a quote from Bob Dole: "At the center of all that afflicts our schools is a denial of free choice." The platform emphasized that school choice includes both private and religious schools by its support for "family choice at all levels of learning" and "urge[d] state legislators to ensure quality education for all through programs of parental choice among public, private, and religious schools."[37]

One favored method of the religious right for protecting their children from the perceived anti-Christian attitudes of public schools is home schooling. For parents who cannot afford a private religious school or do not live near a religious school that meets their needs, home schooling is an important option. The 1996 Republican platform stated that parental choice "includes the option of home schooling and Republicans will defend the right of families to make that choice."[38]

For the religious right, the abortion and education planks of the Republican platform are more important than economic issues. In fact, Reed stated that the Christian Coalition adopted the strategy of supporting the economic concerns of moderate Republicans in exchange for their support of cultural issues. For the Christian Coalition, success in implementing its goals, Reed believes, requires political compromise and adjustment to political reality.[39] Underlying the willingness to compromise over economic goals is a central belief among members of the religious right that improvement in social and economic conditions can result only from improvement in cultural conditions. Therefore, the key to understanding the religious right's focus on schools is its belief in the power of ideas. From the perspective of the religious right, the problem is that a liberal elite controls the dissemination of ideas in U.S. society.

Today the Christian Coalition, through its headquarters in Washington, DC, maintains close tabs on legislation. It immediately alerts its membership about any bill in Congress that is important to the interests of its members. Members are given the postal and e-mail addresses and the fax and telephones numbers of their Congressional representatives so that they can express their viewpoints on pending legislation. However, the real political activity is in local churches. This raises the issue of religious involvement in politics.

In 2001, the Christian Coalition provided the following justification for blending religion and politics. The organization's Web site argues that

> During the 20th Century many Christians vanished from the public policy arena. Post World War II prosperity, along with a desire to avoid becoming "worldly," lured many Christians into political complacency. Unfortunately, the further Christians removed themselves from the political arena, the more our nation's institutions decayed. By the time the danger to our once-great institutions was recognized, the bright lights of the nation once known as the shining "City on a Hill" began to dim. President John Adams said, "Our Constitution was made only for a moral and religious people. It is wholly inadequate to the government of any other." Our nation's foundation was laid upon the bedrock of Biblical truths, truths clearly evident throughout our founding documents. Clearly, our nation's founding fathers expected people of faith to participate in the political process.[40]

Of course, political activity threatens the tax-exempt status of churches. Therefore, the Christian Coalition provides a carefully crafted list of do's and don't's. In the official words of the organization, "And although a church's tax status does limit the amount of political activity it may engage in, it does not prohibit a church from encouraging citizenship."[41] The Christian Coalition informs ministers that the provided list of "do's and don'ts will help guide you, without jeopardizing your church's tax-exempt status, as you lead your congregation into the God-given duties of citizenship. Remember, as Edmund Burke warned, 'All that is necessary for the triumph of evil is for good men to do nothing'."[42]

The Christian Coalitions's list of permissible political actions by churches provides an actual guide to the methods ministers can use to influence their congregations. The Christian Coalition provides ministers with the following instructions:

What Churches May Do

- Conduct non-partisan voter registration drives
- Distribute non-partisan voter education materials, such as Christian Coalition voter guides and scorecards
- Host candidate or issue forums where all viable candidates are invited and allowed to speak
- Allow candidates and elected officials to speak at church services; if one is allowed to speak, others should not be prohibited from speaking
- Educate members about pending legislation
- Lobby for legislation and may spend no more than an insubstantial amount of its budget (five percent is safe) on direct lobbying activities
- Endorse candidates in their capacity as private citizens - A pastor does not lose his right to free speech because he is an employee of a church
- Participate fully in political committees that are independent of the church[43]

The Christian Coalition also provides boundaries for the political action of churches:

What Churches May Not Do

- Endorse candidates directly or indirectly from the pulpit on behalf of the church
- Contribute funds or services (such as mailing lists or office equipment) directly to candidates or political committees
- Distribute materials that clearly favor any one candidate or political party
- Pay fees for partisan political events from church funds
- Allow candidates to solicit funds while speaking in church
- Set up a political committee that would contribute funds to political candidates[44]

The combination of the actual organization of the Christian Coalition and the political activity of ministers makes this a powerful organization. It certainly has helped to make pro-family and educational issues a central piece of the current Bush administration.

EVOLUTION VERSUS CREATIONISM

The 2001 decision of the Kansas State Board of Education to reinstate the theory of evolution in the state's science curriculum was another episode in the ongoing struggle by the religious right against evolutionary theory. For Christian fundamentalists, evolutionary theory contradicts the Word of God as literally interpreted from the Bible regarding the creation of humans. So-called "creationists" say a divine being created humans and other species. They say that because evolution cannot be observed or replicated in a laboratory, there is no evidence that it actually occurred. In the Kansas controversy the "big bang" theory, which contends that the universe was born from a vast explosion, had also been dropped from the curriculum.

The Kansas controversy echoed the famous 1920s Scopes trial, in which high school biology teacher John T. Scopes was accused of violating Tennessee's Butler Act, which forbade the teaching of evolutionary theory. Scopes was convicted of violating the law, but the verdict was later reversed on technical grounds by the state supreme court. However, the Butler Act remained in effect until 1967. Other states also have recently been embroiled in the evolution controversy. In Alabama, New Mexico, and Nebraska laws and administrative actions require that evolution be presented as theory that is merely one possible explanation. The Texas, Ohio, Washington, and New Hampshire, and Tennessee legislatures defeated similar bills, including the requirement that teachers also present evidence to disprove the theory. Alabama now requires that biology textbooks contain a sticker calling evolution "a controversial theory some scientists present as a scientific explanation for the origin of living things." The sticker also warns the student that "No one was present when life first appeared on earth. Therefore, any statement about life's origins should be considered as theory, not fact."[45]

To members of the religious right evolutionary theory is more than just a scientific dispute—it goes to the heart of the debate about values. Mark Looy of Answers in Genesis, a religious-right creationist group, said that "Students in public schools are being taught that evolution is a fact, that they're just products of survival of the fittest. There's not meaning in life if we're just animals in a struggle for survival. It creates a sense of purposelessness and hopelessness, which I think leads to things like pain, murder and suicide."[46]

The recent Kansas controversy over teaching evolutionary theory began in 1999, when the Kansas State Board of Education deleted it from the state's science curriculum. Although the action did not forbid schools from teaching the subject, it did remove the topic from the state's science tests. This meant that schools could ignore the theory while teaching biology without any resulting harm to students required to take the state's examinations. The issue originally arose in 1998, when the state board appointed a group of scientists to develop state standards for teaching science. When the standards were reviewed by the board, Steve Abrams, a conservative member of the board and former chairman of the state Republican party, declared it was "not good science to teach evolution as fact."[47] With the help of other religious fundamentalists, he rewrote the standards by deleting two pages on evolution while retaining a section on "micro-evolution" that dealt with genetic changes and natural selection within a species. In addition, Abrams added to the state standards "The design and complexity of the design of the cosmos requires [sic] an intelligent designer."[48] After much debate, the board adopted the rewritten standards by a vote of 6 to 4.

The decision of the Kansas State Board of Education created a political firestorm. Kansas Governor Bill Graves declared the new science standards "terrible" and "tragic," resulting in a split in the state's Republican party, with Gov. Graves supporting the moderate Republicans who favored the teaching of evolution and Kansas Sen. Sam Brownback supporting conservatives who opposed it.[49] The political controversy spilled over into the 2000 primary elections for the state board.

The 2000 primary election for the state board focused on the issue of evolution. Five of the 10 state board seats were to be voted on in the election following the primary. Because at the time Kansas was primarily a Republican state, primary outcomes often determine the final election. Voters, most of whom usually ignore the primary, paid close attention, with some actually switching from the Democratic to Republican parties so that they could vote for moderate Republicans. For instance, Democrat Lois Culver of suburban Kansas City denounced the science standards as an effort to put religion in the schools and declared, "I think this election is so critical to Kansas children that I was compelled to suck it up and change parties."[50] Culver announced her intention to vote for Sue Gamble, a moderate Republican who opposed the board's vote.

Groups outside of Kansas became embroiled in the political dispute. People for the American Way, group organized for the specific purpose of countering the political actions of the religious right, brought Ed Asner to the University of Kansas to re-enact the Scopes trial. Phillip Johnson, a University of California law professor, donated money to conservative candidates who espoused his belief in the "intelligent design" theory.[51]

During the primary election, moderate Republican Greg Musil ran television ads referring to the evolution controversy with the statement, "I'm embarrassed that Kansas is now being called a backward state."[52] Linda Holloway, the incumbent conservative Republican candidate, stated that she believed that evolution had been overemphasized in science teaching. Gamble, Holloway's moderate Republican opponent, declared the science standards "put students at a disadvantage on a national level. You need to know about dinosaurs, the age of the earth."[53] Mary Douglass Brown, another conservative Republican candidate, warned, "There's a lot of money in evolution. To me, it's pseudoscience."[54]

Conservative candidates were defeated in the election. On February 14, 2001, the Kansas State Board of Education reversed its previous decision on evolution by a vote of 7 to 3. However, to placate conservative Christians, the board added to the science standards a statement: " 'Understand' does not mandate 'belief.' "[55] In addition, the document instructed teachers that "While students may be required to understand some concepts that researchers use to conduct research and solve practical problems, they may accept or reject the scientific concepts presented. This applies particularly where students' and/or parents' beliefs may be at odds with the current scientific theories or concepts."[56]

Highlighting the political battles over ideas taught in schools, a warning to teachers was placed in the Kansas science standards that

> Teachers should not ridicule, belittle or embarrass a student for expressing an alternative view or belief. If a student should raise a question in a natural science class that the teacher determines to be outside the domain of science, the teacher should treat the question with respect. The teacher should explain why the question is outside the domain of natural science and encourage the student to discuss the question further with his or her family and other appropriate sources.[57]

The evolutionary controversy in Kansas reflects one aspect of the continuing struggle by the religious right to ensure conformity by public schools to their values. Of course, these actions must be placed in the context of other groups pounding on the school door demanding entry for their ideas and values. The difference in this case might be the size and organization of the religious right as compared to other groups.

SECULAR HUMANISM AND RELIGIOUS FREEDOM

At the local level, strong political pressure has been placed on school boards to protect the children of evangelicals from secular humanism and sex education. According to evangelicals, secular humanism teaches that individuals can reason their way to moral decisions rather than rely on the Word of God. Evangelical Christians do not want children to use reasoning in solving moral dilemmas. Instead, they want strict obedience to the Word of God.

One of the first major court cases involving secular humanism began in 1983 in the schools of Hawkins County, Tennessee, when a local parent expressed concern about a new series of readers published by Holt, Rinehart & Winston. According to the complaint, the books were filled with "minorities, foreigners, environmentalism, women in nontraditional roles, and open-ended value judgments without clear right and wrong answers."[58]

The case attracted the attention of a wide variety of religious groups opposed to the teaching of secular humanism, such as Phyllis Schlafly's Eagle Forum, the National Association of Christian Educators, Citizens for Excellence in Education, Concerned Women for America, Pat Robertson's National Legal Foundation, and the American Family Association. In opposition to these groups was the liberal organization People for the American Way.

Criticism of the textbooks included a wide range of topics under the banner of secular humanism. Believing that unregulated capitalism was God's will, critics objected to suggestions of environmentalism because it led to government intervention in the economy. Protestors objected to teaching religious tolerance because it suggested that other religions were equal in value to Christianity. The teaching of international cooperation, evangelicals argued, could lead to world government, which would mean the reign of the antichrist. They also objected to stories that suggested humane treatment of animals and vegetarianism because God created animals for human use and exploitation. Evangelicals particularly objected to any story suggesting that hunting was wrong. Also, they felt that stories suggesting the depletion of resources and the extinction of species were denying God's promise to meet all human needs. Men and women portrayed in nontraditional roles would, according to protestors, destroy the traditional Christian family in which wives remained at home raising their children. For this reason, they opposed anything that smacked of feminism.[59]

After 4 years of litigation, the Sixth Circuit Court of Appeals ruled that public schools did not have to accommodate religious objections to the Holt, Rinehart & Winston readers. A previous lower court ruling suggested that religious objections to the books could be accommodated by assigning different texts or by teaching reading at home. The final ruling enhanced the power of school boards by requiring children attending public schools to read the books selected by school officials.[60]

In 1987, the National Legal Foundation, affiliated with Pat Robertson's Christian Broadcasting Network, provided support for an Alabama case against public schools teaching secular humanism. Robertson used his television show, *The 700 Club*, to publicize the case as a Christian battle against the antireligious tenets of secular humanism. People for the American Way and the American Civil Liberties Union provided legal opposition to the work of the National Legal Foundation. The case received a great deal of attention when Robertson announced his candidacy for the Presidency in 1988.[61]

The plaintiffs charged that 45 textbooks approved for Alabama schools taught secular humanism. Supporting their case was a consent decree signed by Alabama's Gov. George Wallace stating that the religion of secular humanism should be excluded from Alabama schools. On *The 700 Club*, Robertson quoted Gov. Wallace, who said, "I don't want to teach ungodly humanism in the schools where I'm governor." In turn, Robertson declared that taking secular humanism out of the schools was an issue of "religious freedom."[62]

The primary legal problem for the plaintiffs was proving that secular humanism was a religion. Again, the issue was about textbooks teaching children that they could make their own moral decisions without relying on the authority of the Word of God. In a lower court decision, religious conservative Judge Brevard Hand ruled that secular humanism was indeed a religion and that the use of books espousing secular humanism should be removed from the schools. This decision was reversed by the Eleventh Circuit Court of Appeals, which ruled that the books did not violate the First Amendment: "Rather the message conveyed is one of a governmental attempt to instill in Alabama public school children such values as independent thought, tolerance of diverse views, self-respect, maturity, self-reliance, and logical decision-making. This is an entirely appropriate secular effect."[63]

The Christian Coalition later adopted Robertson's claim that secular humanism, along with school prayer, was an issue of religious freedom. Beginning in the 1980 Presidential election, the Republican Party supported the idea of a constitutional amendment allowing school prayers. Reflecting what was now becoming a historic position for the Republican Party, Haley Barbour, Chairman of the National Republican Committee, stated in 1996 that the Republican Party supported the "right to voluntary prayer in schools ... whether through a constitutional amendment or through legislation, or a combination of both."[64]

In 1994, after failing to achieve a school prayer amendment, the Christian Coalition decided to make what Reed called a "seismic shift" in strategy. Rather than campaigning for school prayer, the decision was made to adopt Robertson's language and support an amendment for religious freedom. Reed argued that an emphasis on religious freedom as opposed to the narrower issue of school prayer would appeal to a broader religious audience. The religious freedom amendment would guarantee the right of religious expression to all people in all public settings.[65]

In addition, the Christian Coalition believes that a religious-freedom amendment would protect the rights of students to express their religious beliefs in the classroom. For instance, a student would have the right to support creationism over evolutionary theory in science classes.

In supporting the religious-freedom amendment Reed described the case of a Tennessee high school student, Brittney Settle, who was failed for turning in an essay on the life of Jesus Christ. Without citing the details of the case, Reed claimed that a federal court upheld the right of the school to flunk the student for her religious beliefs. In reaction to the case, Reed stated, "A religious freedom amendment would protect her, along with unbelieving students who are nervous about being compelled to participate in mandatory religious exercises in public schools."[66]

Reps. Newt Gingrich and Dick Armey promised the Christian Coalition that for its support of Republican candidates they would introduce a proposal for inclusion of religious freedom in the First Amendment. When the House Judiciary Committee held hearings in July 1996 on the proposed changes, members of Americans United for Separation of Church and State and other religious groups held a protest in front of the Supreme Court. The proposed changes to the First Amendment would "protect religious freedom, including the right of students in public schools to pray without government sponsorship or compulsion." In addition, the changes would prohibit state and federal governments from denying anyone "equal access to a benefit, or otherwise discriminate against any person, on account of religious belief, expression, or exercise."[67]

During the hearings, the head of the Judiciary Committee, Republican Rep. Henry Hyde, complained that public school teachers often discriminated against Christians by denying reports and essays on Jesus Christ. "Public school teachers, who accept reports on witches," Hyde explained, "forbid students from writing reports on Jesus. This is madness."[68]

One cynical critic, David Ramage, Jr., president emeritus of the McCormick Theological Seminary, accused the Christian Coalition of wanting to rush the amendments through the House of Representatives so that House members' positions could be included in their fall voting guide. Voting "no" on the religious-freedom changes, Ramage suggested, would be listed in the Christian Coalition's voter guide as "a vote against religious freedom" or a "vote against God."[69]

The Christian Coalition failed to get the language of the religious-freedom amendment into the 1996 Republican platform. Following the pattern established in the 1980 platform, the 1996 Republican platform promised that: "We will continue to work for the return of voluntary prayer to our schools and will strongly enforce the Republican legislation that guarantees equal access to school facilities by student religious groups. We encourage State legislatures to pass statutes which prohibit local school boards from adopting policies of denial regarding voluntary school prayer."[70]

SEX EDUCATION AND PORNOGRAPHY

Besides an interest in the religious content of schooling, the religious right has campaigned against pornography and certain forms of sex education. Again, this concern is based on the principle that ideas, as opposed to material conditions, determine the course of civilization. Reflecting on his experience as a student in a Roman Catholic high school where the Jesuit teachers made the possession of pornography a reason for expulsion, Buchanan explained:

> Far greater harm has come, not only to souls but to nations, from polluted books and evil ideas—racism, militarism, Nazism, Communism—than has ever come from polluted streams or rotten food. With the Bible [the Jesuit teachers] taught that it is not what goes in the stomach that "defiles a man, but what comes out of his mouth."[71]

With regard to sex education, the religious right objects to any curricula that discuss birth control, abortion, or homosexuality. From their perspective, the only legitimate topic is the importance of sexual abstinence prior to marriage.

Evangelical groups pressured the Reagan and Bush administrations to distribute only abstinence-oriented sex education programs. In 1991, for example, the American Civil Liberties Union objected to federal sponsorship of Teen Choice and other groups advocating chastity as the solution to teenage pregnancy, claiming that federally sponsored material was filled with religious references that violated the First Amendment. The material advised teenagers to "pray together and invite God on every date." The ACLU also objected to the statement "God is supreme ... God does exist."[72]

In 1994, religious right groups convinced the Texas Board of Education to demand changes in a health text published by Holt, Rinehart &

Winston. Monte Hasie, a member of the Texas Board of Education, claimed the books "were promoting homosexuality as an acceptable alternative life style and promoting sex as being O.K. if you use a condom. We were going to put *Playboy* and *Penthouse* out of business."[73] After months of hearing testimony from family-planning, antiabortion, gay advocacy, fundamentalist Christian and other groups, the board mandated that the health book and four others under consideration delete toll-free numbers for gay, lesbian, and teenage suicide groups; illustrations of examinations for testicular cancer; and sections on homosexuality. They also asked for inclusion of descriptions of Texas laws against sodomy.

The Christian Coalition's influence on the 1996 Republican platform is clearly evident in its long section on sex education, which emphasizes the importance of sexual abstinence prior to marriage. "We support," the platform stated, "educational initiatives to promote chastity until marriage as the expected standard of behavior."[74] In addition, the platform enunciated its opposition to "school-based clinics, which provide referrals, counseling, and related services for contraception and abortion."[75]

The religious right condemns any instruction or positive statements about homosexuality. For the Christian Coalition and other members of the religious right, homosexuality should be publicly condemned. Buchanan argued that gay men should be blamed for bringing about the AIDS plague. In fact, the Christian Coalition's first membership drive in 1989 focused on the National Endowment for the Arts sponsorship of the homoerotic photographs of Robert Mapplethorpe.[76]

Evident in the 1996 Republican platform are objections to gay and lesbian rights. The platform praised the recently passed Republican-sponsored Defense of Marriage Act. In the words of the platform, this legislation "defines 'marriage' for purposes of federal law as the legal union of one man and one woman and prevents federal judges and bureaucrats from forcing states to recognize other living arrangements as 'marriages.' "[77]

In 1995, the Christian Coalition placed strong political pressure on Congress to censure pornography on the World Wide Web and television. In its effort to remove pornography or, as it is called, *cyberporn*, from the World Wide Web, the Christian Coalition sought the aid of Democrats after Massachusetts Democratic Rep. Edward Markey introduced a bill requiring television manufacturers to install "v-chips" to allow parents to block programs with too much violence.[78]

Working with a group of Democrats and Republicans, the Christian Coalition claimed a major responsibility for the writing of the 1995 Telecommunications Act requiring censorship of cyberporn and v-chips. Reed believes that passage of the telecommunications legislation moved the Christian Coalition from simple criticism of legislative action to the exercise of legislative power. Reed and other coalition members sat down with members of Congress and worked out the details of the telecommunications legislation.

The work on the telecommunications bill demonstrated that the Christian Coalition could influence both political parties. Reed argues that the relationship between evangelical Christians and the Republican Party is simply strategic. "The two are not one and the same," he stated. "Indeed, the partnership between the profamily movement and the GOP is less a romance than a shotgun wedding."[79]

MULTICULTURAL EDUCATION

Another major area of concern for the religious right is multicultural curricula. Evangelical Christians do not believe, as mentioned before, in teaching tolerance of other religions. For evangelicals, Christianity is the only true religion. In addition, the religious right believes that the Judeo–Christian foundation of American culture makes it superior to other cultures. Therefore, instruction should emphasize the inculcation of Judeo–Christian culture and not tolerance for other cultures.

In 1986, William Bennett made a name for himself in academic circles when he launched a public attack against the Stanford University faculty for replacing a freshman undergraduate course entitled "Western Culture," in which students read 15 works in Western philosophy and literature, with a course entitled "Cultures, Ideas, and Values," in which readings would include works by "women, minorities, and persons of color."[80] Bennett argued that students should be required to study Western culture because it provides the framework for American government and culture. In addition, he stated, "Probably most difficult for the critics of Western culture to acknowledge is that 'the West is good'." Western culture, according to Bennett, has "set the moral, political, economic, and social standards for the rest of the world."[81]

In 1994, issues of religion, sex, and multiculturalism came together in a bitter struggle among the governor of California, the state legislature, and educators over a proposed statewide test for grades K–12. The storm over the test, originally called the *California Learning Assessment System test* and later the *California Comprehensive Assessment System*, erupted when author Alice Walker and the People for the American Way objected to state education officials removing from the test two of Walker's stories.

One story, "Roselily," was removed because of objections by the Traditional Values Coalition, a religious right organization. The story dealt with a Christian woman in rural Mississippi marrying a Muslim, and it was considered antireligious. Beverly Sheldon, research director for the Traditional Values Coalition, argued that the test would influence the religious values of students.

The other story by Walker was removed because a member of the state board of education considered it hostile to meat eating. As mentioned previously in the discussion of the Tennessee case, evangelicals believe God put animals on earth to be eaten and exploited by humans.

The People for the American Way objected to the removal of the stories because it sent "a chilling message across the country of the threat to educational freedom and constitutional rights posed by extremist pressure groups."[82]

By May of 1994, hundreds of people were turning out for school board meetings throughout California to support or protest the test. Some of the protests were about a rumored question depicting a barber contemplating the slitting of a customer's throat. A Los Angeles school board member, Sue Stokka, objected on the basis that the test did not emphasize basic skills. A temporary restraining order against giving the test in the San Bernadino school district was issued by a superior court judge after a suit was filed by the conservative Rutherford Institute. The school board in the Antelope Valley Union High School district voted not to give the test.

By September of 1994 the test was a major political issue. Gov. Pete Wilson, who was running for re-election in November, threatened to veto a reauthorization of the testing program. A new objection to the test program was raised when a study found that men, Latinos, and Asian Americans were underrepresented among the groups that developed the test questions. A new legislative bill called for the exclusion of all questions related to personal beliefs regarding family life, gender, and religion.[83]

The religious right's stance against multiculturalism is reflected in the 1996 Republican platform's call for an emphasis in schools on teaching about Western civilization and its pledge to make English the official language of the United States. The platform vowed to create an education consumer's warranty which, among other things, would guarantee that all American children would "learn the nation's history and democratic values and study the classics of Western civilization."[84] In addition, the platform proposed that "To reinforce our American heritage ... [states and local school boards require] our public schools to dedicate one full day each year solely to studying the Declaration of Independence and the Constitution."[85] With regard to the language issue, the platform clearly stated: "We support the official recognition of English as the nation's common language."[86]

Reed recognized that many Republicans and Democrats do not share the Christian Coalition's religious interest in school choice, secular humanism, sex education, and multiculturalism. However, many Republicans recognize the importance of the religious right's voting power. Although he supported Republicans in the 1994 Congressional contest, Reed was disappointed that many concerns of the religious right were not included in the Contract With America, a political statement drafted by right-wing Republicans. But, thinking like a practical politician, Reed hoped that "success on the Contract with America ... would build the political capital necessary to gain passage of other legislative initiatives dealing with abortion and school choice."[87]

LIBERAL DOMINATION OF EDUCATION
AND CULTURE

There is a strong populist rhetoric running through the statements of the religious right. Even New Democrats claim that they want to reduce the power of the federal government and return the control of public institutions to the people. Arguments for school choice emphasize breaking the stranglehold of an educational bureaucracy and returning power over schooling to parents. A great deal of the rhetoric is antigovernment and filled with complaints that government agencies and bureaucrats represent a third class that for its own benefit has seized power from the people.

This rhetoric was evident in the acceptance speech of Vice Presidential candidate Jack Kemp, at the 1996 Republican convention. Kemp charged that Democratic opponents were elitists who "don't have faith in the people. They have faith in government."[88] Although Kemp, in his speech, was primarily concerned with economics, he was playing on the supposed dislike of the general public for government policies created by bureaucratic experts and then forced on an unsuspecting populace.

Many in the religious right believe the liberal elite is composed of both cultural and government leaders. William Bennett argued that the cultural war is between the beliefs held by most citizens and "the beliefs of a liberal elite that today dominates many of our institutions and who therefore exert influence on American life and culture."[89] This liberal elite, according to Bennett, inhabits universities, the literary and artistic worlds, liberal religious institutions, and the media. The liberal elite, according to Bennett, is different from former bourgeois elites, who valued the importance of the family, public morality, hard work, and individual entrepreneurship. In contrast, the liberal elite rejects many traditional Christian values and looks with scorn on Americans who believe in the value of hard work and economic individualism. Furthermore, this liberal elite supports ideas that are anathema to the religious right, such as multiculturalism, sexual freedom, and gay and lesbian relationships.

From the perspective of the religious right, it is the combination of government bureaucrats and the liberal elite that is responsible for imposing unwanted government policies and values on the public. For instance, southern Whites and northern ethnic Whites—the important new constituencies in the Republican Party—showed open resentment for school desegregation, particularly for the method of forced busing. From their viewpoint, desegregation policies were forced on them by a liberal Supreme Court and liberal educational bureaucrats and were supported by liberal elites living in suburbs protected from the effects of integration.

For religious fundamentalists, it was a combination of a liberal Supreme Court and liberal government bureaucrats that replaced prayers and Bible reading in public schools with secular humanism. As the religious fundamentalists see it, a combination of liberal writers and educational bureaucrats have forced textbooks on schools that undercut evangelical values. From this perspective, it is the influence of liberal cultural elites that results in textbooks containing the values of vegetarianism, one-worldism, and secular humanism. It is liberal elites who promote sex education programs filled with teaching about birth control, homosexuality, and AIDS. It is liberal elites who are responsible for the sexuality and violence in movies and television programs that, from the perspective of the religious right, undermine family values and increase crime rates.

It is important to understand that the resentment against the so-called liberal elite and government bureaucrats is based on real policies that were, in fact, imposed on many unwilling citizens. This does not mean that these policies were wrong but that they were not initiated by the communities most affected by them. In reality, there do exist government officials, legal experts, and media elites who do not represent the values of the religious right and segregationists. Therefore, the opposition to educational and government bureaucrats and the desire to return power to the people is based on the assumption that this will restore traditional values to education.

CONCLUSION

As Michael Lind wondered, is the culture war a smoke screen for growing economic inequalities? Are northern and southern White workers simply blaming cultural and racial changes for a decline in real income? Should northern and southern White workers be focusing their attention on the redistribution of wealth as opposed to cultural issues?

Whether the culture war is a smoke screen for the increasing economic inequalities in U.S. society or a result of a growing sense of alienation and disadvantage among White workers, the result is a sharp political debate about U.S. schools. School choice and privatization could cause major structural changes in education. Issues of evolution, secular humanism, sex education, multiculturalism, and affirmative action will continue to contribute to political divisiveness.

NOTES

1. Molly Ivins and Lou Dubose, *Shrub: The Short But Happy Political Life of George W. Bush* (New York: Random House, 2000), 60–63.
2. "Off to a Quick Start," *Education Week on the Web*, 14 February 2001. Available: www.edweek.org
3. Joetta L. Sack, "New Secretary Has a Playbook for Motivating Students," *Education Week on the Web*, 14 February 2001. Available: www.edweek.org
4. Kathleen Manzo, "Drilling in Texas," *Education Week on the Web*, 10 June 1998, 1. Available: www.edweek.org
5. Sack, "New Secretary."
6. Ibid.
7. "Educational Policy Statement of Bush Campaign," retrieved from http://www. georgebush.com, 24 August 2000.
8. Marvin Olasky, *Renewing American Compassion* (Washington, DC: Regnery, 1997), 41–42.
9. Ibid., 36.
10. Ibid., 29–30.
11. Ibid., 28.
12. George W. Bush, Comment on the front cover of Myron Magnet, *The Dream and the Nightmare: The Sixties' Legacy to the Underclass* (San Francisco: Encounter Books, 2000).
13. Magnet, *The Dream*, 20.
14. Ibid., 24.
15. Patrick J. Buchanan, *Right From the Beginning* (Washington, DC: Regnery Gateway, 1990), 14.

16. Michael Lind, *Up From Conservatism: Why the Right Is Wrong for America* (New York: The Free Press, 1996), 154.

17. Ibid., 161.

18. Buchanan, *Right From the Beginning*, 6. Emphasis in quote is Buchanan's.

19. William J. Bennett, *The De-Valuing of America: The Fight for Our Culture and Our Children* (New York: Simon & Schuster, 1992), 36.

20. Joel Spring, *The American School*, 5th ed. (New York: McGraw-Hill, 2001), 58–133.

21. Bennett, *The De-Valuing of America*, 206.

22. Ralph Reed, *Active Faith: How Christians Are Changing the Soul of American Politics* (New York: Free Press, 1996), 9.

23. This message is given on the Christian Coalition's Web site, http://cc.org/about.html.

24. See Jacob Weisberg, *In Defense of Government: The Fall and Rise of Public Trust* (New York: Scribner's, 1996), and Michael Tomasky, *Left for Dead: The Life, Death and Possible Resurrection of Progressive Politics in America* (New York: Free Press, 1996).

25. See Joel Spring, *The American School: 1642–1993* (New York: McGraw-Hill, 1994), 406–407, 412–414.

26. Reed, *Active Faith*, 105.

27. Jacob Weisberg, "Fear and Self-Loathing," *New York* (19 August 1996), 36.

28. Ibid., p. 36.

29. Reed, *Active Faith*, 4, 11.

30. Buchanan, *Right From the Beginning*, 6.

31. Reed, *Active Faith*, 109–111.

32. Reed, *Active Faith*, 111.

33. 1996 Republican Party Platform as released over the Republican World Wide Web site on 13 August 1996, p. 15.

34. Alan Elsner, "Evangelicals Assert Control of Republican Party," Compuserve Executive News Service, Reuters Ltd., 7 August 1996, 1.

35. Ibid.

36. 1996 Republican Platform, 21–23.

37. Ibid., 21.

38. Ibid.

39. Reed, *Active Faith*, 188–235.

40. Christian Coalition, http://cc.org.

41. Ibid.

42. Ibid.

43. Ibid.

44. Ibid.

45. Pam Belluck, "Kansas Votes to Delete Evolution From State's Science Curriculum," *New York Times on the Web*, 12 August 1999. Available: www.nytimes.com

46. Ibid.

47. Ibid.

48. Ibid.

49. Pam Belluck, "Board Decision on Evolution Roils an Election in Kansas," *New York Times on the Web*, 29 July 00. Available: www.nytimes.com

50. Ibid.

51. Ibid.

52. Ibid.

53. Ibid.

54. Ibid.

55. John W. Fountain, "Kansas Puts Evolution Back Into Public Schools," *New York Times on the Web*, 15 February 2001. Available: www.nytimes.com

56. Ibid.

57. Ibid.

58. Joan Delfattore, *What Johnny Shouldn't Read: Textbook Censorship in America* (New Haven, CT: Yale University Press, 1992), 14.

59. Ibid., 36–60.

60. Ibid., 61–75.

61. Ibid., 76–79.

62. Ibid., 81.

63. Ibid., 87.

64. Haley Barbour, *Agenda for America: A Republican Direction for the Future* (Washington, DC: Regnery, 1996), 159.

65. Reed, *Active Faith*, 117–118.

66. Ibid., 118.

67. See Eric Schmitt, "Church Leaders Split on Plan for School Prayer Amendment," *New York Times*, 24 July 1995, A16, and Jim Luther, "School Prayer," Compuserve Executive News Service, Associated Press, 22 July 1996, 1.

68. Schmitt, "Church Leaders," 16.

69. Ibid.

70. 1996 Republican Platform, 21.

71. Buchanan, *Right From the Beginning*, 339; Reed, *Active Faith*, 131.

72. Laurie Asseso, "Teen Chastity," Compuserve Executive News Service, No. 2120, 17 February 1991.

73. Sam Dillon, "Publisher Pulls a Textbook in Furor on Sexual Content," *New York Times*, 17 March 1994, B10.

74. 1996 Republican Platform, 21.

75. Ibid.

76. Buchanan, *Right From the Beginning*, 339; Reed, *Active Faith*, 131.

77. Ibid., 20.

78. Reed, *Active Faith*, 229–231.

79. Ibid., 234.

80. Bennett, *The De-Valuing of America*, 170.

81. Ibid.

82. Karen Diegmuller, "Removal of Literary Works From California Test Stirs Flap," *Education Week*, 9 March 1994, 11.

83. Karen Diegmuller, "Model Exam in California Is Target of New Attacks," *Education Week*, 4 May 1994, 1, 12.

84. 1996 Republican Platform, 21.

85. Ibid.

86. Ibid., 17.

87. Reed, *Active Faith*, 185.

88. Adam Nagourney, "Kemp Gives Early Look at Strategy," *New York Times*, 15 August 1996, A24.

89. Bennett, *The De-Valuing of America*, 26.

Chapter 2

Think Tanks, Neoconservatives, and the Libertarian Party: Marketing School Choice and National Standards

◆ ◆ ◆

"Conservative foundations are investing wisely to bring their clearly artic-ulated vision of America into being," warned Carole Shields, president of People for the American Way. She went on to say, "Their success is trou-bling ... because there is no equivalent funding pattern to support a more progressive vision."[1] Twenty years before Shields's warning, I got caught in the web of conservative think tanks that were financing scholars and using marketing methods to spread ideas about school choice, privatiza-tion of public education, and home schooling. By the late 1980s, these think tanks added national academic standards to their educational agenda. In the 1990s, they gave financial aid to reactionary scholars such as Richard J. Hernstein and Charles Murray to write *The Bell Curve: Intel-ligence and Class Structure in American Life*. And in 2001, President George W. Bush entered the White House with the backing of the Manhattan Institute and favoring its educational policies.

THE MANHATTAN INSTITUTE AND BUSH'S EDUCATIONAL POLICIES

Under the banner "Turning Intellect Into Influence," the Manhattan In-stitute's Web site proudly lists its influence on Bush's administration. First on the list are two carriers of the torch of conservative compassion-ism as preached by Marvin Olasky and supported by the institute. The Manhattan Institute's John Dilulio was appointed Director of the White House Office of Faith-Based and Community Initiatives, and Stephen Goldsmith was named Special Advisor to the President for Faith-Based and Community Initiatives. Influence on economic policy was ensured by the institute's former Senior Fellow Lawrence Lindsay acting as Chief Economic Advisor to Bush and the appointment of the Institute's David Frum as Special Assistant to the President for Economic Speech Writing. While at the Institute, Lindsay wrote the book that influenced Bush's tax policies: *The Growth Experiment: How the New Tax Policy Is Transforming the U.S. Economy*. The institute's influence on civil rights issues was assured by the appointment of Senior Fellow Abigail Thernstrom to the U.S. Commission on Civil Rights. Also, of course, the institute cited Senior Fellow Myron Magnet's book *The Dream and the Nightmare ...* [as] 'The book that helped shape Bush's message'."[2]

The Manhattan Institute's influence on national educational policies involves an amalgamation of politics and think tank intellectuals. The Manhattan Institute is a nonprofit organization that funds scholarly work for the purpose of influencing public policy. "The Manhattan Institute," the opening line posted on its website declares, "has been an important force in shaping American political culture."[3] This is followed by the statement "We have supported and publicized research on our era's most challenging public policy issues: taxes, welfare, crime, the legal system, urban life, race, education, and many other topics."[4]

Even more revealing of its open use of scholarship to promote certain political and educational causes is the statement accompanying its plea for donations. Written by the institute's trustee, Walter Wriston, the contribution form contends that "The Institute's intellectual capital far exceeds its financial capital, making it the most cost-effective organization of its kind. Although the impact of our ideas dwarfs our financial resources, we still need the latter. There is not a better bargain to be had."[5] At the bottom of the form the contributor is asked if he or she wants to receive e-mail updates on "Education Reform," "Welfare Reform," "Crime Reduction," "Faith-Based Initiatives," "Race and Ethnicity Initiatives," and "Legal Reform."[6]

Educational policy was Bush's topic when he spoke at the Manhattan Institute during the 2000 primary campaign. At the institute, Bush was warmly greeted as "my homeboy" by former congressman Rev. Floyd Flake.[7] In this tangled web of connections, Flake had, just before introducing Bush, accepted the headship of the charter school division of the Edison Schools Inc., the largest for-profit school-management company in the country. Flake is listed on the "Education Reform" section of the institute's Web site along with former U.S. Department of Education Assistant Secretaries Chester E. Finn, Jr., and Diane Ravitch as being "at the forefront of today's thinking about how our children's educational achievement can be increased."[8] Finn is identified on the Web site as the John M. Olin Fellow at the institute. I have more to say about Finn, Ravitch, and the Olin Foundation later in this chapter.

Bush's proposal to give vouchers to parents of children in failing schools closely parallels the policies promoted by the Manhattan Institute. During the 2000 campaign, the Republican Party platform advocated the empowerment of "needy families to escape persistently failing schools by allowing federal dollars to follow their children to the school of their choice."[9] Bush and Republican leaders contemplated that parents whose children were in schools that consistently had failing test scores would be given the choice of using federal Title I funds to send their children to private schools. This plan was similar to the one praised in the Manhattan Institute's publication on Florida's A-Plus accountability and school choice program, operated under the leadership of George W. Bush's brother, Gov. Jeb Bush. The institute's report, authored by Jay P. Greene, claimed that "By offering vouchers to students at failing schools, the Florida A-Plus choice and accountability system was intended to motivate those schools to improve .... This report found that students' academic test scores improve when public schools are faced with the prospect that their students will receive vouchers."[10]

At a 1999 luncheon at the Manhattan Institute, Jeb Bush described what he called the "Bush/Brogan A+ Plan for Education" in the following words: "In Florida today, every school is graded on an A through F scale. We said that when a school has been rated F for two out of four years, that school would be defined as a failure, and the parents in those schools would be given other options." One of the options Bush described were scholarships that "would enable [parents] to choose a private school for their child, religious or non-religious, so long as the private school admitted all applicants, accepted the opportunity scholarship amount as full tuition, and used the same standardized tests as used by our public schools.[11]

Vouchers are a target area on the Manhattan Institute's educational agenda. With the objective of influencing public debate, the institute's official program description states that "Educational reform is the top public policy concern today, so it should come as no surprise that the Manhattan Institute has the best education reform experts in the country to offer *practical advice to policymakers*."[12] Also, as part of its research agenda, the institute is focusing on vouchers as a method for helping low-income parents escape public schools.

The institute's research on vouchers is not a search for truth but a search for justifications for its political program. An objective research

program would seek to find out if vouchers are an effective means of improving school conditions. However, the institute's program statements
indicate a belief that vouchers are the solution: "One of the most important areas of research for our experts *will be the need* for school vouchers
… Vouchers … *would both improve educational performance* and give the
existing public school bureaucracy an incentive to make dramatic
changes in their schools in order to keep parents satisfied."[13]

Therefore, the goal of the institute's support of research is not to prove
whether vouchers are effective but to create arguments supporting
voucher plans. Objective research is replaced by political polemics. This
is most evident in the institute's efforts to effect public opinion through
marketing its educational experts to the media. Using its contacts in the
media, the Manhattan Institute ensures that its paid scholars will be contacted for their opinions on educational policies. This results in the frequent appearance of their experts' names in newspaper stories. The institute proudly keeps track of its media influence and lists it on its Web site
under the categories of "National Media Attention" and "Press Releases."
Examples of the effectiveness of these efforts can be found in daily newspapers. For instance, when the *New York Times* reported on threatened
teachers' strikes, there appeared the following comment: " 'Some of the
reforms that bear on teachers are beginning to gain some traction on the
ground, and teachers' organizations don't like that at all,' said Chester E.
Finn Jr., an education expert at the Manhattan Institute, a conservative
research organization."[14] The Manhattan Institute is opposed to the work
of teachers' unions. When Massachusetts students protested state testing,
the *New York Times* reported, " 'What we are asking for is knowledge
that any student who wants a high school diploma worth the paper it's
written on should have,' said Ms. Thernstrom, a senior fellow at the
Manhattan Institute, a conservative research group. 'All other measures
are subjective.' "[15] Along with George W. Bush, the institute supports
statewide testing of students. When Donald G. and Doris Fisher, owners
of The Gap clothing chain, announced they were providing $15 million
in seed money to nationally franchise KIPP charter schools, the *New York
Times* reported, " 'We've got brand-names for everything else,' observed
Chester E. Finn Jr., an education analyst at the Manhattan Institute.
'Now we have Comer schools and Hirsch schools, and we're going to
have KIPP schools and Edison schools—You're going to be able to move
into a new city and say, "Show me the local Hirsch school." That's not a
bad idea for a modern mobile society.' "[16] The institute supports both
charter schools and privatization of public schools.

The combination of the Manhattan Institute's attempts to affect public policy and the work of politicians is even evident in higher education. In 1998, New York City Mayor Rudy Guiliani appointed a seven-member task force to prepare a plan for reforming the City University of New York. Reflecting his conservative Republican views, Guiliani selected as chair of the task force Benno Schmidt, Jr., who was head of the Edison Project—the same private school corporation that would later select Manhattan Institute's Floyd Flake to lead its charter school division. Another member of the task force was Heather MacDonald, a John M. Olin fellow at the Manhattan Institute.[17]

Another method of the institute is to pay newspaper reporters to attend so-called informational meetings. For instance, the institute, along with the American Enterprise Institute, provided research money to Herrnstein and Murray to write *The Bell Curve*, a book that purports to show the intellectual inferiority of lower social classes and African Americans. After the completion of the book, the institute provided honoraria of $500–$1,500 to influential politicians and journalists to attend a seminar on Murray's research.[18]

The Manhattan Institute's association with *The Bell Curve* highlights some of the inherent racism in conservative arguments. A group of studies used in *The Bell Curve* was supported by the Pioneer Fund, which has been criticized for the politics of its 1937 founder, Wyckliffe Draper. Draper, a textile tycoon, was an admirer of the eugenics policies of Nazi Germany. After World War II, the Pioneer Fund provided major financial support to psychologist Arthur Jensen and physicist William Shockley, who argued that innate genetic inferiority was the cause of Black poverty and failure in school.[19]

Murray's defense for using research supported by the Pioneer Fund is stated thus:

> Never mind that the relationship between the founder of the Pioneer Fund and today's Pioneer Fund is roughly analogous to that between Henry Ford and today's Ford Foundation. The charges have been made, they have wide currency, and some people will always believe that *The Bell Curve* rests on data concocted by neo-Nazi eugenicists.[20]

My interest is not in the statistical data used by Herrnstein and Murray to argue—I am a softheaded type who believes statistics can be manipulated to support any belief—that Whites and African Americans differ by an average of 15 IQ points. I am interested in their program recommendations, which are similar to those of other Manhattan Institute policies. For instance, Herrnstein and Murray argued that "These [differences in average IQ scores] are useful in the quest to understand why ... occupational and wage differences separate blacks and whites, or why aggressive affirmative action has produced academic apartheid in our universities."[21]

Herrnstein and Murray argued that affirmative action results in bringing many African American students onto college campuses who are unable to academically compete with White students. As a result, many African American students separate themselves from the rest of the student body and support Black Studies departments. This is what Herrnstein and Murray mean by "academic apartheid." Their answer to current affirmative-action policies is to treat people as individuals and to apply the same standards to all students. They also believe that the current form of affirmative action results in the dumbing down of curricula and textbooks and the spread of multiculturalism.

Herrnstein and Murray contended that the financial and social elite of society deserve their social positions because of their superior average IQs. With regard to educational policies, their concern is not with the average student, who they feel receives an adequate education commensurate with his or her IQ, but with the gifted student. In language that reflects their intellectual elitism and educational concerns, they contended:

> It needs to be said openly: The people who run the United States—create its jobs, expand its technologies, cure its sick, teach in its universities, administer its cultural and political and legal institutions—are drawn mainly from a thin layer of cognitive ability at the top .... It matters enormously not just that the people in the top few centiles of ability get to college ... or even that many of them go to elite colleges but that they are educated well.[22]

Basing their view on this reasoning, Herrnstein and Murray argued for the concentration of educational programs on the needs of the gifted. Furthermore, in one of the most unusual arguments for school choice, they proposed that the federal government support school choice because parents of gifted children will be the type that will select a tougher academic program. In fact, they argued that because IQ is inherited, educational ambition is primarily "concentrated among the parents of the brightest of the brightest. Policy [referring to school choice] should make it as easy as possible for them to match up with classes that satisfy their ambitions."[23]

Although the policymakers of the Manhattan Institute are associated with these racist and elitist views, I do not want to infer that they are directly reflected in the educational policies of George W. Bush. However, the belief held by President Bush and other compassionate conservatives that the poor are poor because of their moral standards rather than economic conditions could be labeled elitist and a form of cultural imperialism. On the other hand, there is a direct connection between the educational policies of the Bush administration and the policies advocated by the Manhattan Institute.

THINK TANKS, FREE MARKET IDEOLOGY, AND SCHOOL CHOICE

The work of Manhattan Institute and its effects on the Bush presidency is only one example of how think tanks influence public policy. During the 1970s, the religious right's demands for school choice paralleled the extreme free-market ideas advocated by conservative think tanks. These free-market ideas included ending all government intervention in education and support of schooling and turning education over to the competition of the marketplace. This radical form of capitalism had its origins in Austria in the late 19th century.

In the 1950s, Friedrich Hayek, Austrian economist and later Nobel Prize winner, moved to the United States and taught at the University of Chicago from 1950 to 1962. Hayek influenced a number of American economists, including Murray Rothbard, William Simon, and Milton Friedman. In their most radical anarcholibertarian form, Austrian economists such as Rothbard advocated abolishing all forms of government and applying free-market theory to every aspect of living, including highways, law enforcement, defense, and schooling.[24] Without government interference, these Austrian economists argued, marketplace competition would create ideal institutions. Applied to schooling, this meant no government provision or control of education. Instead, entrepreneurs would organize schools and compete for students while the "invisible hand" of the marketplace determined what forms of schooling were best.

Hayek's economic ideas played a major role in the Reagan-style Republicanism of the 1980s and 1990s and in conservative attacks on liberalism and government bureaucracy. In the 1930s, Hayek debated English economist John Maynard Keynes over the role of government in a capitalist system. Keynes argued that for capitalism to survive governments needed to intervene in the economy. Classical liberals, such as John Stuart Mill, opposed government intervention, but the progressive liberals of the 1930s justified government intervention to ensure equality of oppor-

tunity and provide a social safety net as necessary for the survival of capitalism.[25]

In *The Road to Serfdom* Hayek set the stage for later conservative criticisms of government bureaucracies, including educational bureaucracies.
He argued that the difficulty of determining prices or the value of goods
would inevitably cause the failure of centrally planned economies. According to Hayek, pricing determines the social value of goods: What
should a car cost in relation to food? What should the price of health
care be in relation to education? In a free market, Hayek asserted, prices
or social values are determined by individual choice. In a planned economy, pricing or social value is determined by a government bureaucracy.
What criterion is used by a government bureaucracy? Hayek's answer was
that the inevitable criterion is one that promotes the personal advantage
of bureaucracy members. In addition, bureaucrats and intellectuals supported by a bureaucracy will advance social theories that vindicate the
continued existence and expansion of the bureaucracy.[26]

Defining the enemy as the bureaucracy is one of Hayek's enduring leg-
acies. Many educational critics complain that the problem with public
schools is the educational bureaucracy. A frequently heard statement regarding schools is: "The problem is not money! The problem is bureaucratic waste!" By placing the blame on the educational bureaucracy,
school reformers can avoid the issue of equal funding among school districts. Some public school students receive the benefits of living in well-
financed suburban school districts, whereas others languish in overcrowded classrooms in poorly funded school districts that lack adequate
textbooks and educational materials. Blaming the bureaucracy became an
easy method for avoiding increased educational funding.

Beginning in the 1950s and lasting through the 1990s, conservatives
claimed that a major problem is control of schools by a self-serving educational bureaucracy. In addition, as discussed in chapter 1, right-wing
Republicans insist that a liberal elite controls the culture of universities,
public schools, and the media. Hayek identified this liberal elite as a new
class composed of government experts and their intellectual supporters.
Within this framework schools could improve only if the power of the educational bureaucrats were broken and schools functioned according to
the dictates of market competition.

Friedman, a colleague of Hayek's at the University of Chicago and
1976 Nobel Prize winner, became the first American, at least to my
knowledge, to advocate the use of vouchers as a means of providing
school choice. In contrast to Rothbard, Friedman argued that the benefits of maintaining a stable and democratic society justified government

support of education, but not government-operated schools. Friedman proposed a government-financed voucher that parents could redeem "for a specified maximum sum per child per years if spent on 'approved' educational services."[27] Friedman believed the resulting competition between private schools for government vouchers would improve the quality of education.

With arguments similar to those heard in the 1990s that vouchers or tuition tax credits would improve the quality of education, Friedman contended in the 1960s that vouchers would overcome the class stratification that results from the existence of rich and poor school districts. As Friedman suggested, "Under present arrangements, stratification of residential areas effectively restricts the intermingling of children from decidedly different backgrounds."[28] Except for a few parochial schools, Friedman argued, private schools were too expensive for most families, which resulted in further social class divisions in education.

Like Friedman, many U.S. conservatives embraced the concept of the free market but rejected the idea of completely abandoning government control, particularly social and moral control. After the riots and student rebellions of the 1960s and 1970s, conservatives believed that the government should exercise moral authority over social life but, accepting the idea of the free market for business, they believed that the government should not interfere in the economy.

Maintaining that a liberal elite controlled universities and government bureaucracies, conservatives felt they needed to create what William Simon, head of the John Olin Foundation, called a *counterintelligentsia* to spread free-market economic ideas, including the ending of the public school monopoly over education.[29] The financing for this counterintelligentsia would come from privately supported think tanks.

PLANNING AN INTELLECTUAL REVOLUTION: THE TRICKLE-DOWN THEORY OF IDEAS

I remember being told in the early 1970s, at a meeting at the Institute for Humane Studies in Menlo Park, California, that conservatives were organizing a cadre of intellectuals to openly support freedom and capitalism because colleges and universities were hopelessly controlled by left-wing intellectuals. I was one of those academics, the right hoped, who could be persuaded to spread libertarian and conservative ideas into academic establishments and to policymakers. Being elitists, these conservatives wanted to focus their efforts on intellectual and political leaders. Just as supply-side economists would later talk about trickle-down economics, these conservatives believed in trickle-down ideas.

At the time, I did not understand this to be part of a movement later described by James Smith in his 1991 book *The Idea Brokers*: "In the early 1970s, executives in a handful of traditionally conservative foundations redefined their programs with the aim of shaping the public policy agenda and constructing a network of conservative institutions and scholars."[30] One of the leaders and articulate spokespersons of this movement was William Simon, who left his job in 1976 as Secretary of the Treasury in the Nixon and Ford administrations to become head of the John Olin Foundation, the purpose of which, in Simon's words, "is to support those individuals and institutions who are working to strengthen the free enterprise system."[31]

Reflecting Simon's economic beliefs, the preface and foreword for his book *A Time for Truth* were written, respectively, by Friedman and Hayek. In the preface, Friedman sounded the warning that intellectual life in the United States was under the control of "socialists and interventionists, who have wrongfully appropriated in this country the noble label 'liberal' and who have been the intellectual architects of our suicidal course."[32] Applying concepts of the marketplace to intellectual life, Friedman argued that the payoff for these "liberals" was support by an entrenched government bureaucracy. In other words, the liberal elite and the government bureaucracy fed off each other. Using a phrase that would be repeated by conservatives throughout the rest of the 20th century, Friedman contended that "the view that government is the problem, not the cure," is hard for the public to understand.[33] According to Friedman's plea, saving the country required a group of intellectuals to promote a general understanding of the importance of the free market.

To undermine the supposed rule of a liberal intelligentsia, Simon urged the business community to support intellectuals who advocate the importance of the free market. Simon called on businesspeople to stop supporting colleges and universities that produced "young collectivists by the thousands" and media "which serve as megaphones for anticapitalist opinion." In both cases, Simon insisted, businesspeople should focus their support on university programs and media that stress procapitalist ideas.[34]

In his call for action, Simon calculated that the first step should involve businesspeople rushing "multimillions to the aid of liberty, in the many places where it is beleaguered." On receiving the largesse of business, he insisted, "Foundations imbued with the philosophy of freedom . . . must take pains to funnel desperately needed funds to scholars, social

scientists, writers, and journalists who understand the relationship between political and economic liberty."[35]

In light of Simon's remarks as head of the John Olin Foundation in the
1970s, it is interesting that two of the leading writers for the conservative
cause in education, Finn and Dinesh D'Souza, are, respectively, John
Olin Fellow and scholar at the Hudson Institute and the American Enterprise Institute. Besides scholars at the conservative Hudson Institute
and the American Enterprise Institute, the John Olin Foundation, with
assets of $90 million, backed many right-wing causes and, according to
one writer, "its pattern of giving became [in the 1970s] more sophisti-
cated and more closely attuned to the potential of grantees for influencing debates on national politics."[36]

Although conservatives talk about the invisible hand of the free market, the trickle-down distribution of ideas is very well planned. For the
antipublic school movement and other items on the right-wing agenda,
the following methods are used.

1. Creating foundations and institutes that fund research and policy
   statements supportive of school choice, privatization of public schools
   and, more recently, charter schools.
2. Identifying scholars to conduct research, write policy statements,
   and lecture at public forums that are favorable to school choice, privatization of public schools, and charter schools.
3. Financing conferences to bring like-minded scholars together for the
   sharing of ideas and the creation of edited books.
4. Paying scholars to write newspaper opinion pieces that are then distributed to hundreds of newspapers across the country.

This fourth point is an important element in the trickle-down theory
of ideas. It is a big leap from writing a research report to being featured on
the opinion–editorial page of the New York Times or other leading newspapers. As I discuss later in this chapter, this frequently occurs with con-
servatively backed educational commentators, such as Finn and Ravitch.

It requires connections and a public relations staff to gain quick access
to the media. Providing this type of access is one of the important elements in the strategy of spreading the conservative agenda. With public
relations help from conservatives, I appeared in the 1970s as an "academic expert" on radio and television shows across the country. On one
occasion, after the exercise portion of an early morning television show, I

fielded call-in questions ranging from "Why can't my daughter read?" to "Why are all college professors socialists?" There was never any hint that my appearance on the program resulted from the work of conservative and libertarian organizations.

In *The Transformation of American Politics: The New Washington and the Rise of Think Tanks*, David Ricci described the attempt to mobilize and control public opinion. "Those who talked about developing conservative ideas," Ricci stated, "were committed not just to producing them but to the commercial concept of a product, in the sense of something that, once created, must be placed before the public as effectively as possible."[37]

THE LIBERTARIAN PARTY: WALKING AMONG THE POT-SMOKING NUDIST RIGHT

In Milwaukee, Wisconsin, on November 16, 1972, I had my first encounter with the world of funding that would eventually sell the conservative dream to the American public. At the time, I was the proud author of my recently published doctoral dissertation, "Education and the Rise of the Corporate State," and an assistant professor scrambling to make a living and accumulate the academic points required for tenure and promotion. Therefore, I was quick to accept an invitation, sizable honorarium, and travel expenses to present a paper on compulsory education in Milwaukee.

In my rush to accept, I did not pay much attention to the names of the two sponsoring organizations: the Center for Independent Education and the Institute for Humane Studies. My book attracted the attention of these two organizations because it concluded that the only hope for a free society was to separate schooling from the control of the state. I had reached this conclusion after noting that in the early 20th century a variety of groups—including corporations, labor unions, socialist organizations, and political parties—wanted public schools to shape students into their image of the good citizen. I didn't feel that a democratic society could exist if the state used schools to control the minds of their citizens. The only 20th-century critics of this attempt to control the public through schooling were anarchists such as Emma Goldman. Attracted to Goldman's politics and those of other anarchists, I proclaimed myself, in the spirit of the rebellious 1960s and early 1970s, an anarchist.

In the early 1970s, my self-proclaimed anarchism was not repugnant to Austrian economists such as Rothbard, who argued that the political spectrum was a circle with the right and left meeting at one point. This meeting point, according to Rothbard, was the recognition that the state was the enemy. To individuals on the extreme left the state was the enemy because it was used by corporations and financiers as a tool for increasing and protecting their wealth. This is now called *corporate welfare*. To individuals on the free-market right the state was the enemy because it was used by communists and fascists to destroy freedom and individualism. From this perspective, a prime enemy of both extremes was the public school, which, according to the left was used to spread an ideology that protects those with wealth, and according to right was used to indoctrinate students into the principles of collectivism.

In his presentation at the Milwaukee conference, Rothbard concluded by noting that both the liberals, such as Henry Barnard and Horace Mann, and the conservatives, such as members of the Ku Klux Klan, supported public over private schooling. In the case of the Klan Rothbard referred to the 1920 Klan-controlled Oregon state legislature, which, because of the Klan's anti-Catholicism and opposition to private Catholic schools, passed a law requiring all children to attend public schools. The law was struck down in the 1920s in the U.S. Supreme Court decision *Pierce* v. *Society of Sisters*, with the declaration "The child is not the mere creature of the state." Rothbard concluded that "the *Pierce* decision points the way to a fundamental choice that must eventually be made with respect to public compulsory schooling in America: either Pierce and liberty or Horace Mann and the Ku Klux Klan."[38]

The conference proceedings, published as *The Twelve Year Sentence: Radical Views of Compulsory Schooling,* were edited by William F. Rickenbacker, a longtime advocate of a return to a metal standard for currency and a senior editor of William F. Buckley Jr.'s conservative magazine the *National Review*. Echoing Rothbard, Rickenbacker applauded the idea of conservatives casting their nets to the left to capture potential left-wing adherents to conservative causes. He approvingly wrote in the introduction, "Some come at [compulsory education] with the value sets and presuppositions of the conservative right, others of the anarcho–capitalist or traditional Liberal or New Left positions."[39]

At the conference I met Chuck Hamilton, now an editor at the Liberty Fund in Indianapolis, who asked if I had any manuscripts I wanted to have published. Using a recent inheritance, he was starting a publishing house in New York. After the conference, I sent him my manuscript, *Radical Forms of Education*, which he retitled A *Primer of Libertarian Education*, a book he then distributed around the world. Just happy to be published, I signed a contract giving all my royalties to some unspecified anarchist institute.[40]

After the Milwaukee conference I received frequent invitations to visit the Center for Independent Education, located in San Francisco. At the center I met John Coons, whose book, coauthored with William Clune and Stephen Sugarman, provided the first detailed plan for a voucher sys-tem to finance school choice.[41] At this time, the center's work focused on spreading the idea of school choice and school vouchers, and preparing a California referendum for vouchers. The center also provided legal advice to Christian fundamentalists interested in breaking the hold of public schools.

In the 1970s, the Center for Independent Education maintained a close relationship with the journal *Libertarian Review* and the Cato Insti-tute, which were both located near the Embarcadero in San Francisco. At this time, the Libertarian movement was characterized by an open flaunting of the law. I remember editors and staff at the *Libertarian Review* sitting at their desks dipping their pipes into humidors filled with mari-juana and puffing their way to a free society. While on a speaking tour in southern California, I was headquartered at a Libertarian nudist home in Newport Beach, California, where evening gatherings took place in a heated pool and Jacuzzi amid air filled with rock music, television, and the aroma of pot.

By the 1980s, the free spirit of the movement came to an end as con-servative donors tightened their nets and discarded the radical cultural elements that had been caught. The Cato Institute packed its bags and moved to Washington, DC, where it provided position papers on cutting taxes and downsizing government for Reaganites and members of the Bush administration. Always interested in ending public schooling, the Cato Institute opened one of its recent publications, *Liberating Schools: Education in the Inner City*, with an article entitled "The Public School Monopoly: America's Berlin Wall," by David Boaz, executive vice presi-dent of the institute. Other articles in the book were written by John Coons, who has continued to be recycled by conservatives, and more re-cent advocates of school choice, John Chubb and Terry Moe, who authored the 1990 book *Politics, Markets & America's Schools*. Moving in this world of think tank scholarship, Chubb and Moe's research was sponsored by the Brooking Institute.

The Cato Institute's continuing support of school choice and free-mar-ket economics is clearly reflected in Boaz's opening article in *Liberating Schools*. After stating the usual conservative charge that the educational bureaucracy has ruined public schools, Boaz proposed "a program of vouchers or education tax credits ... [that] will give families the clout that valued customers have. Schools will compete to attract them. Par-ents will be more involved in their children's education .... Businesses will be able to hire the educated workers that a world-class economy in the information age demands."[42]

By the middle of the 1980s, my invitations to libertarian and conservative conferences on education came to an end. My work proved less appealing to the right as I focused on the role of schooling in causing and maintaining economic inequalities in the global economy. Rather than the cultural and democratic freedom I envisioned, which from my perspective required economic equality, the conservative and libertarian organizations were primarily influencing policies that were making the rich even richer or, in different words, increasing the wealth of donors to conservative think tanks.

Of course, it is not surprising that the public statements and proposed policies emerging from conservative think tanks support the economic interests of their donors. It is hard to imagine large groups of wealthy donors supporting scholars and their research that results in promoting suicidal policies—at least for the wealthy—of economic equality and redistribution of wealth.

My realization that I was being manipulated by money while working at the Center for Independent Education and the Cato Institute resulted in a lifelong vow, which I have kept, of never accepting another grant from a private foundation or government agency. In the 1970s, when I asked where the money was coming from to support lavish conferences, organization offices, travel expenses, honoraria, and public relations, I was told it was a gift from a "friend of liberty" who earned his money by practicing "liberty-loving economic policies." Well, this "friend of liberty" turned out to be David Koch, who inherited, along with his brother Charles, a fortune from his father, Fred Koch, a founder of the ultraconservative John Birch society. Koch industries are the second largest family-owned business in the United States, with annual sales of $20 billion. Each brother is listed by *Forbes* as among the 50 wealthiest Americans. The Koch brothers continue to provide the major backing for the Cato Institute.

Probably very few Americans have ever heard of David and Charles Koch. Unlike Ross Perot, most conservative backers of think tanks prefer to stay out of the public spotlight. The Koch brothers' behind-the-scenes manipulation of scholars and research has an important impact on public opinion. From my personal experience during the 1970s, the Center for Independent Education, the Cato Institute, and the Institute for Humane Studies played major roles in raising public awareness about issues of school choice and school voucher systems and in creating a hostile climate for public schools and educational bureaucrats.

In the 1990s, the Libertarian Party was not as interested in school issues as it had been in former years. The 1996 Libertarian national campaign platform still promoted separation of school and state within the context of complete freedom from the government. The preamble to the 1996 platform declared that "libertarians stand for individual liberty, self-responsibility, and freedom from government—on all issues at all times."[43]

Libertarians reject all government financing of education, including the funding of school choice plans by vouchers or tuition tax credits. Parents will be able to make a school choice for their children, the writers of the 1996 platform reasoned, with the repeal of the income tax. The Libertarian platform stated:

> The most effective way we can improve education in America is to repeal the income tax, so that you can afford to educate your child your way—in a private school that offers the curriculum you want, in a religious school that teaches the values in which you believe, or through home-schooling conducted your way.[44]

The Libertarian platform dismisses the educational proposals of the Democrats and Republicans as attempts to impose a social agenda on the U.S. population.

The Libertarian Party still believes that complete freedom of ideas is essential for the progress of society. Consequently, they support complete freedom of education so that there is a diversity of competing ideas in the marketplace. This complete freedom allows the marketplace to determine which ideas are of most value. Government intervention, from their perspective, results in particular interest groups trying to impose their ideologies on children through a public school system. The Libertarian position is in sharp contrast to that of neoconservatives, who want to maintain the moral and social authority of government over education while letting the marketplace determine the best methods for inculcating government-supported ideologies.

NEOCONSERVATIVES: ACADEMIC STANDARDS, CHOICE, AND CHARTER SCHOOLS

Neoconservatives, as compared to traditional conservatives, can be thought of as a blend of the religious right and Austrian economics. For traditional conservatives, the government's major social roles are protecting the workings of capitalism, maintaining a social safety net, and ensuring public morality. For instance, Presidents Eisenhower and Nixon can be placed within this conservative tradition. President Eisenhower supported public housing projects as a social safety net because of their potential to stabilize capitalism by reducing the tensions between the rich and the poor.

In contrast, neoconservatives, influenced by Austrian economics, believe traditional government programs should be privatized or controlled by the workings of a free market. Putting their faith in the power of a free market to improve lives, they reject the idea of government providing social safety nets such as welfare and health care. However, neoconservatives believe that government should play an active role in protecting public morality and the quality of schooling through government censorship and academic standards.

Backed by a network of foundations, neoconservatives Denis Doyle; Chester Finn, Jr.; and Diane Ravitch combine free market economics and the necessity for government standards in their public messages about education. Because they spend most of their time working for the federal government and foundations, they have achieved a presence in the popular media far beyond the capabilities of academics in universities and colleges. For instance, those familiar with "American education's newspaper of record," *Education Week*, or the op-ed pages of *New York Times* have probably noticed educational articles frequently reporting the opinions of these three educational neoconservatives.

A major source of their financial backing and public relations support comes from the Hudson Institute. Founded in 1961 by Herman Kahn, who gained a national reputation for his books *On Thermonuclear War* and *Thinking the Unthinkable*, the Hudson Institute was primarily supported by contracts from the Department of Defense and the Office of Civil Defense. After Kahn's death in 1983, the institute relocated from Croton-On-Harmon, New York, to Indianapolis, Indiana. Backed by the Lilly Endowment and the local business community, the Hudson Institute now focuses on a variety of neoconservative issues.[45]

The board of trustees of the Hudson Institute includes former Vice President Dan Quayle, one of the political favorites of right-wing Republicans. Also on the board is Mitchell E. Daniels, Jr., president of Eli Lilly and Company, which finances the Lilly Endowment. The Lilly Endowment provides major support for both the Hudson Institute and the ultraconservative American Enterprise Institute. The president of the Hudson Institute, Leslie Lenkowsky, is also a resident fellow of the American Enterprise Institute.[46]

Bruno Manno, a senior fellow at the Hudson Institute, was appointed Assistant Secretary of Education by President George Bush in 1992.

Manno worked with Secretary of Education Lamar Alexander, also a senior fellow at the Hudson Institute, in creating Goals 2000. According to
the biographical sketch released by the Hudson Institute, "Dr. Manno . . .
directed the work of the team that created America 2000 [later called
Goals 2000]."[47]

Manno is also featured in the Heritage Foundation's book *The Insider*.
The Heritage Foundation is an important part of the right-wing maze. In
The Insider, Manno criticizes outcome-based education for not focusing
on academic outcomes but on outcomes defined by educators who "emphasized values, attitudes and behavior, and often reflect quasi-political
or ideologically correct positions."[48]

The Insider also features another senior fellow at the Hudson Institute:
Denis Doyle, who is also an analyst for the Heritage Foundation. The
Hudson Institute's World Wide Web page in 1996 featured Doyle as
their first "Who's Who in Education Land?" entry. Like Manno, Doyle
moves in the shadowy world of neoconservative think tanks and government agencies. Besides his government employment, Doyle lists his jobs
as senior fellow at the Heritage Foundation and as an American Enterprise Institute Fellow.[49] Holding a master's degree in political theory,
Doyle has coauthored books on education with some of the corporate
elite, including David Kearns, CEO of Xerox and former Assistant Secretary of Education, and Louis Gerstner, Jr., CEO of IBM and RJR
Nabisco.[50]

With Gerstner, Roger Semerand, and William Johnston, Doyle coauthored *Reinventing Education: Entrepreneurship in America's Public Schools*.
At the time of the book's publication, Semerand was on the board of
trustees of the Hudson Institute, and Johnston was a senior fellow at the
Hudson Institute. Reflecting the belief that the free market is the cure for
many institutional problems, the authors blamed the problems of public
schooling on government bureaucracies. Their book claims that "the real
meaning of choice in education is to harness the most powerful aspect
of the market, the voluntary coming together of willing buyers and sellers. Just as we choose our elected officials, our houses of worship, the
stores and shops we patronize, so too, should we be able to select our
schools."[51]

Doyle's compatriots at the Hudson Institute, Finn and Ravitch,
founded the Educational Excellence Network in 1982, which continues
as a project of the Hudson Institute. The network bills itself as a national
clearinghouse for educational information and expert advice. The "We
believe" section of the Network's World Wide Web home page lists the
following neoconservative credo for education:

1. Every young American needs an education with a solid academic core ... and a healthy dose of "cultural literacy."
2. Dramatically higher expectations are necessary for U.S. children and schools.
3. American education should be driven—and judged—by unswerving adherence to standards, legitimate academic outcomes, and accountability.
4. The education system should be designed and operated to meet the needs of its consumers rather than the interests of its producers. One way to bring this about is through "civilian control" of key policy decisions.
5. Every school needs teachers who know their subjects ... and [are] held accountable for what their students learn.
6. The public requires a steady flow of timely and clear information about the performance of the education system.
7. We can learn from other countries—and should welcome opportunities to compare ourselves and compete with them in education as in other domains.[52]

The Educational Excellence Network recently provided a flood of educational policy statements and "briefings, legislation monitoring, policy analysis, and expertise to policymakers, educators, business groups, and community leaders."[53] The "Hot Topics" section of the Educational Excellence Network is dominated by the writings of Finn and Ravitch. In August 1996 two articles were offered by Finn: "Charters, Charters, and Charters" and "Making Standards Matter 1996." In June 1996 there were four articles by Finn, seven articles by Ravitch, and one by Mike Garber, and in July 1996 three articles were offered by Ravitch and one by Finn.[54]

Finn's 1996 article on charter schools provides a good example of how the media are used as part of the trickle-down theory of influencing public opinion. In early August 1996, I downloaded from the Hudson Institute's World Wide Web page Finn's article on charter schools.[55] Shortly afterward, I turned to the op-ed page of New York Times and found a bold title across the top: "Beating Up on Charter Schools," by Finn, who was identified as a Fellow of the Hudson Institute and former Assistant Secretary of Education during the Reagan administration. In the article, Finn attacked the two teachers' unions—favorite targets of the right—for hindering the growth of charter schools.[56]

Finn also provides a good example of foundation-based scholars who are used by conservatives to implement their trickle-down theory of ideas. After earning his doctorate in education policy and administration at Harvard University, Finn became a professor of education at Vanderbilt University in 1981 and, while on leave from Vanderbilt, he served in a variety of government positions before becoming Assistant Secretary for Research and Improvement as well as counselor to Secretary of Education William Bennett from 1985 to 1988. After Bush replaced Reagan as president, Finn returned to Vanderbilt. In 1992, while on another leave from Vanderbilt, Finn joined Chris Whittle's Edison Project as a founding partner and senior scholar. The Edison Project, as I discuss later, has been a source for ideas about charter schools and privatization of public education. In 1994, while still on leave from Vanderbilt, Finn was appointed John M. Olin Fellow at the Hudson Institute.[57]

Ravitch is another foundation-based scholar. Never holding a full-time academic appointment until recently—she was an adjunct professor at Teachers College, Columbia University in the 1980s—Ravitch served as Assistant Secretary of Education as well as counselor to the Secretary of Education from 1991 to 1993. Besides her continuing work with the Hudson Institute, she is now a senior research scholar at New York University and a senior Fellow at the Manhattan Institute.[58] In 1989, the Manhattan Institute established the Center for Educational Innovation for the promotion of school choice plans. The Center for Educational Innovation's World Wide Web page states that: "Our mission is to transform public education in America by shifting accountability from centralized bureaucracies to local schools and by creating systems of school choice for communities."[59]

With the support of these think tanks, Finn and Ravitch have flooded the market with neoconservative opinions about education. Besides more than 200 articles in professional and popular journals, Finn has written 10 books, including *Radical Education Reform*, *We Must Take Charge: Our Schools and Our Future*; and *Scholars, Dollars and Bureaucrats*. With Ravitch, Finn coauthored *What Do Our 17-Year-Olds Know?* Ravitch has also written more than 200 articles for the popular and scholarly press, and 6 books, including *National Standards in American Education: A Citizen's Guide 1995*, *The Schools We Deserve*, and *The Great School Wars: New York City, 1805–1973*.[60]

The neoconservative philosophy of Finn and Ravitch, with its combination of free market thinking and the use of government authority to impose social order, is captured in a statement by Finn in a review of a book advocating the libertarian position of complete separation of school and state. In reference to complete abolition of the government's role in education, Finn stated, "I don't share the author's hostility to standards, curricula and assessments set by policymakers, but I resonate with his ideas about freeing schools from state control of management and freeing families to select the education that suits them."[61]

In a similar fashion, Ravitch has argued that the academic standards of public schools declined in the 1960s and 1970s as a result of demands by civil rights groups for equality of educational opportunity and because of the capitulation of educational administrators to student rebels. Reacting to the permissiveness of the 1960s and 1970s, Ravitch believes the key to school improvement is the re-establishment of educational authority through imposition of government academic standards and achievement tests.[62]

In their coauthored report, "Education Reform 1995–96," Finn and Ravitch made a distinction between systemic reform and reform based on reinvention. Systemic reform, as they defined it, involves federal and state governments creating academic standards and assuming responsibility for their implementation. Reinvention, on the other hand, involves federal and state governments establishing academic standards with actual implementation of these standards left to the free market. "The reinventing model we favor," they stated, "is not a wide-open, unbridled free market."[63] The authority, they reason, should remain with the government to ensure that all students receive a quality education.

Within the framework of reinventing schools, Finn and Ravitch leveled three criticisms at the federal government. First they contended that federal policies are still based on the problems of the 1960s, when minority and disabled students were blatantly discriminated against. Today, they argued, the problems are quite different and involve "mediocrity, under-performance, low standards, slavish adherence to ineffective instructional strategies, and a rigid, bureaucratized, producer-oriented, one-size-fits-all delivery system."[64] They consider the $7.2 billion authorized in 1996 for Title I a waste of money. Instead, they propose that money for Title I could be turned into vouchers given to state and local governments. Second, they believe that federal educational spending primarily feeds an overexpanded bureaucracy.

Like Bennett and other right-wing critics, Finn and Ravitch argue that federal programs are controlled by a liberal elite. Despite the fact that all three of these critics held important government positions in the Office of Education, Finn and Ravitch charged, that "federally funded R&D centers at elite colleges of education are a major factory for the dissemination and replenishment of the one-sided progressive philosophy."[65] Similar to other right-wing politicians and educators, they are opposed to multicultural and bilingual education. They refer to the federal government's support of bilingual education as a "politicized program."[66] In contrast to their desire for immediate Americanization of immigrants, they stated, "Many bilingual educators are more interested in sustaining the ethno–linguistic, cultural, and political distinctiveness of immigrant populations than in their rapid assimilation into the mainstream."[67]

In their assessment of the 1996 election Finn and Ravitch expressed worry that Republicans will forget about the issues of "discipline, standards, uniforms, charter schools, accountability."[68] Political candidates, they emphasize, need to maintain the authority of government in the areas of discipline, standards, and accountability, while supporting "consumer-oriented" reforms such as school choice.

For Finn and Ravitch, government should wield a big stick to ensure that the invisible hand of the free market produces schools that meet the academic expectations of neoconservatives. What would happen if the free market created schools that taught ideologies that threatened the wealth of the donors to the Hudson Institute and other conservative think tanks?

There has been recent criticism of the assumption that high academic standards and achievement tests will overcome educational problems. Jonathan Kozol suggested in *Savage Inequalities* that poor academic performance in urban schools could be the result of insufficient money to provide complete sets of textbooks, well-equipped science laboratories, good counseling, and well-trained teachers.[69] For instance, high academic standards will not solve the problems of New York City public schools which, because of student overcrowding in 1996, had to operate classrooms in a converted World War II torpedo factory, a renovated department store, aluminum trailers, and in school hallways and auditoriums. The New York City schools were worse off in 1996 when compared with conditions Kozol described in 1991.[70] In addition, there is a continuing debate over the effectiveness of progressive education that focuses on student interests instead of traditional instruction using "high" academic standards. Although this debate continues without any clear winners, it does call into question the idea that high standards and testing will improve schools.[71]

The claim that U.S. schools are academic failures is also being challenged. Michael Lind calls the charge that public schools are academic failures one of the "three conservative hoaxes" of modern times. Lind wrote, "Thanks to a decade and a half of well-coordinated conservative propaganda, many Americans have been persuaded that America's public schools are miserable failures and that American students are among the worst in the industrialized world. Those who believe these assertions, it turns out, have been misled."[72]

In *The Manufactured Crisis: Myths, Fraud, and the Attack on America's Public Schools*, David Berliner and Bruce Biddle argued that the conservative hoax began in the 1980s, when the Reagan administration issued the report *A Nation at Risk*, which claimed the American economy was failing because of its public schools. Countering *A Nation at Risk*, Berliner and Biddle provided statistics showing that U.S. students taking courses similar to those of students in other countries, such as Japan and Germany, do as well or, in some cases, better, and that it is the comprehensiveness of the student body in U.S. public schools that tends to lower overall scores. Berliner and Biddle argued that not until the appearance of *A Nation at Risk*, did neoconservatives such as Bennett, Finn, and Lynne Cheney launch their attacks on public schools.[73]

THE HERITAGE FOUNDATION AND THE AMERICAN ENTERPRISE INSTITUTE: MARKETING RACISM AND SCHOOL REFORM

The Heritage Foundation, often called the General Motors of conservative think tanks, published Finn and Ravitch's 1995 report on school reform in their monthly general *Policy Review*. In the same issue appeared an article by Dinesh D'Souza, who at the time was the John Olin scholar at the American Enterprise Institute.[74] D'Souza's article, "We the Slaveowners: In Jefferson's America, Were Some Men Not Created Equal?", provides an upbeat note to American slavery with the interesting conclusion that "Slavery was an institution that was terrible to endure for slaves, but it left the descendants of slaves better off in America. For this, the American Founders are owed a measure of respect and gratitude."[75]

The Heritage Foundation and the American Enterprise Institute, the two largest right-wing think tanks, provide an example of the interconnections within the neoconservative world. First, as I noted previously, both Finn and D'Souza are supported by the John M. Olin Foundation. Second, these scholars and think tanks support similar policies regarding multiculturalism and academic standards. With research and writing supported by the American Enterprise Institute and the John Olin Foundation, D'Souza's 1991 book, *Illiberal Education: The Politics of Race and Sex on Campus*, criticizes affirmative action and multicultural education.[76] Attacking the supposed domination of politically correct thinking on American college campuses, D'Souza argued that affirmative action is both destructive of both minority students and the quality of education. Affirmative action, he argued, results in colleges admitting many poorly prepared minority students. "The consequence," he claimed, is "minority students placed in 'high risk' intellectual environments where they compete against vastly better-prepared students, and where their probability of graduation is known to be low."[77] D'Souza also believes that multiculturalism and feminism are destroying liberal education by causing the replacement in college courses of significant books written by White men with inferior books written by minorities and women.

In *Policy Analysis* the range of articles from other right-wing foundation scholars illustrates the Heritage Foundation's overall goal of being a disseminator of neoconservative ideas. One of the organizers of the Heritage Foundation, Edwin Fuelner, referred to it as a "secondhand dealer in ideas."[78] The Heritage Foundation had its origin in a plan developed by Pat Buchanan at the request of President Nixon. Shortly after Nixon's 1972 election, Buchanan proposed the creation of an institute that would be a repository of Republican beliefs and would provide a Republican talent bank for conservative thinkers. Buchanan, along with Fuelner and Paul Weyrich, solicited $250,000 in financial support from Joseph Coors, the Colorado brewer and supporter of conservative causes. Opening its doors in 1973, the Heritage Foundation received further support from the John Olin Foundation and John Scaife, a Mellon heir and another supporter of conservative causes.[79]

After the 1980 election the Heritage Foundation presented President Reagan's White House transition team with a 1,000-page volume entitled *Mandate for Change*. The volume, which summarized neoconservative thinking about a broad range of issues, including education, set the tone and direction of the Reagan administration.

Currently, the Heritage Foundation influences politicians and the general public through the dissemination of neoconservative ideas. In 1995, the Heritage Foundation prepared a special report for congressional appropriations committees recommending the elimination of 34 categorical programs in the Department of Education, including public library construction and library literacy programs. In other federal programs related to education, the Heritage Foundation called for the elimination of Indian elementary and secondary education and the Women's Educational Equity Fund for Improvement of Education. Pursuing its goal of creating school choice, the Heritage Foundation recommended that "Congress should also alter the expansive Title I program, perhaps giving the money directly to poor parents in the form of educational vouchers that they can then use at the school of their choice."[80]

In contrast to the dissemination role of the Heritage Foundation, the American Enterprise Institute focuses on supporting neoconservative scholarship. Originally organized in 1943 to educate the public about business, the American Enterprise Institute dramatically changed in the 1960s under the leadership of William J. Baroody, who applied the concepts of Austrian economics to the world of ideas. Baroody believed there existed a liberal monopoly of ideas. Later, neoconservatives such as Bennett and Buchanan referred to this liberal monopoly as the work of the "liberal elite" or "liberal establishment." Baroody argued that "a free society can tolerate some degree of concentration in the manufacture of widgets. But the day it approaches a monopoly in idea formation, that is its death knell."[81]

Baroody proposed creating a free market of ideas by breaking the liberal monopoly through the establishment of conservative think tanks. Once competition was created, he believed, the invisible hand of the marketplace would determine the value of particular ideas. During the early 1970s, Melvin Laird, Secretary of Defense in the Nixon administration, kicked off a $25 million fundraising campaign for the American Enterprise Institute in a Pentagon dining room. By the 1980s, the institute had a staff of 150 and an annual budget of more than $10 million.

In the 1990s, evidence of the American Enterprise Institute's success at introducing conservative thinking into the marketplace of ideas is illustrated in Peter Brimelow's afterword to his anti-immigration book *Alien Nation*. Brimelow, writer for the conservative *Forbes* magazine, recalled in his afterword to the paperback edition of his book an incident at an American Enterprise Institute ceremony in which Judge Robert Bork commented, "We at [the American Enterprise Institute] are grateful to you for drawing fire away from Charles Murray."[82] (The other author of *The Bell Curve*, Richard Herrnstein, died shortly after completion of the manuscript.) Brimelow commented about Bork's remarks, "Later . . . I got a call from Murray himself, Bork's colleague at [the American Enterprise Institute] . . . curious to see how I was holding up [from the stormy reaction to the publication of *Alien Nation*]."[83] Also, reflecting the web of conservative connections, Brimelow acknowledged intellectual and financial support from the Cato Institute and William F. Buckley of the conservative *National Review*, where Brimelow had originally published his immigration argument in a 1992 cover story.[84]

Brimelow's book supports right-wing and racist ideas regarding immigration. In *Alien Nation* Brimelow expressed concern about the decreasing percentage of Whites in the U.S. population. Arguing that U.S. citizens have a legitimate interest in the racial composition of their population, Brimelow commented, "The American nation of 1965, nearly 90 percent white, were explicitly promised that the new immigration policy would not shift the country's racial balance. But it did ... [and] it seems to me that they have a right to insist that it be shifted back."[85] The result of shifting racial patterns, Brimelow claims, is a destruction of national unity and cultural homogeneity. To solve this problem, he proposed closing the gates to immigrants for several years and, when they are reopened, using racial balance and labor market needs as criteria for selecting new immigrants.

Brimelow argues that the shift in racial and cultural composition of the population resulted in strong support for affirmative action, bilingual education, and multicultural education. These policies, he feels, put Whites at an unfair disadvantage in the labor market and are causing a disintegration of traditional U.S. culture. Like other scholars of the right, Brimelow wants multiculturalism replaced with Americanization programs based on traditional American values and the implementation of an English-only national language policy. In Brimelow's words, "All diversion of public funds to promote 'diversity,' 'multiculturalism' and foreign-language retention must be struck down as subversive."[86]

CONCLUSION

In agreement with the religious right, conservative think tanks are marketing the idea of school choice by financing conservative-oriented research and by using public relations methods to influence media, politicians, and the general public. They have provided intellectual justification for the religious right's inherent racism and fear of the cultural changes resulting from immigration. However, the work of neoconservative think tanks also highlights an important difference between neoconservative thinkers and the religious right. The religious right rejects the idea of government imposing national academic standards and testing. They want to rely on the authority of God. School choice would provide the religious right with this opportunity. In contrast, neoconservatives, such as Doyle, Finn, and Ravitch, believe that school choice will create more efficient ways of implementing government-established national academic goals and standards. This neoconservative viewpoint received support in the educational policies of George W. Bush, who as governor of Texas included in his agenda testing and vouchers for parents of children in failing schools.

It is important to emphasize that a conscious effort is being made to disseminate ideas and influence public opinion by conservative think tanks, such as the Hudson Institute, the Manhattan Institute, the Heri-

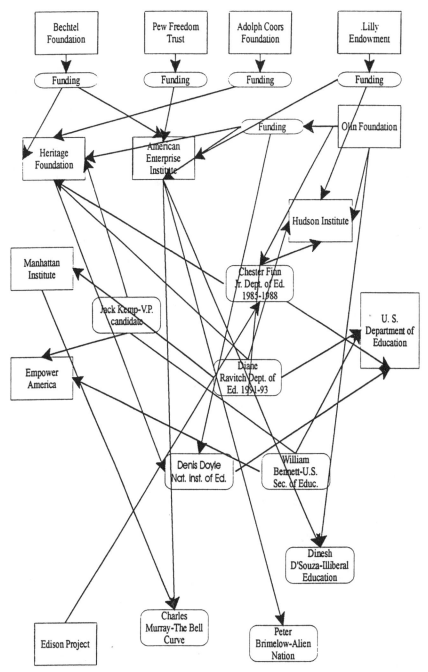

FIG. 2.1. The web of conservative think tanks in education.

tage Foundation, and the American Enterprise Institute. Their influence is the result of calculated planning by conservative intellectuals and businesspeople.

In 1986, at a celebration of the accomplishments of the Heritage Foundation, President Reagan recognized the importance of conservative attempts to influence public opinion. After paying homage to Austrian economists Friedrich Hayek and Ludwig von Mises, Reagan recalled the argument made by Richard Weaver in the 1948 book *Ideas Have Consequences*. Reagan told those celebrating of the work of the Heritage Foundation: "It goes back to what Richard Weaver had said and what Heritage is all about. Ideas do have consequences, rhetoric is policy, and words are action."[87]

Besides giving public recognition to the importance of Austrian economics and conservative foundations, President Reagan in 1981 appointed the longtime advocate of school vouchers Milton Friedman to his Economic Policy Advisory Board. Reagan also selected William Simon, the architect of the conservative counterintelligensia, to chair his Productivity Commission. The "Reagan revolution" in many respects represents the triumph of Austrian economics and the work of conservative think tanks.

Figure 2.1 partially illustrates the web of conservative think tanks that have a major influence on educational policy.

NOTES

1. "Buying a Movement: New Report Analyzes Right-Wing Foundations," People for the American Way Web Page, p. 3. Available: www.pfaw.org
2. "Manhattan Institute for Policy Research," Manhattan Institute Web site, http://www.manhattan-institute.org/.
3. "About Manhattan Institute," Manhattan Institute Web site, http://www.manhattan-institute.org.
4. Ibid.
5. "Sponsoring the Manhattan Institute," Manhattan Institute Web site, http://www.manhattan-institute.org.
6. Ibid.
7. Edward Wyatt, "Floyd Flake to Take Post With Education Company," *The New York Times on the Web*, 3 May 2000.
8. "Program Areas: Educational Reform," Manhattan Institute Web site, http://www.manhattan-institute.org.
9. Republican National Committee, "Education and Opportunity: Leave No American Behind," Republican National Platform. Available: www.rnc.org/2000/2000platform3.

10. "An Evaluation of the Florida A-Plus Accountability and School Choice," Manhattan Institute Web site, http://www.manhattan-institute.org.

11. Jeb Bush, "Civic Bulletin 22: Achievement and Opportunity: Keys to Quality Education." Available: http://www.manhattan-institute.org.

12 "Program Areas: Educational Reform," Manhattan Institute Web site, http://www.manhattan-institute.org. Italics added.

13. Ibid., italics added.

14. Steven Greenhouse, "Autumn of Teachers' Discontent Is Dawning," *The New York Times on the Web*, 20 September 2000. Available: www.nytimes.com

15. Jacques Steinberg, "Blue Books Closed, Students Protest State Tests," *The New York Times on the Web*, 13 April 2000. Available: www.nytimes.com

16. Jodi Wilogoren, "Seeking to Clone Schools of Success for Poor," *The New York Times on the Web*, 16 August 2000. Available: www.nytimes.com

17. "Who's Who at CUNY," *The New York Times on the Web*, 6 May 1998. Available: www.nytimes.com

18. Michael Lind, *Up From Conservatism: Why the Right Is Wrong for America* (New York: Free Press, 1996), 182.

19. Lind, *Up From Conservatism*, 197.

20. Richard J. Herrnstein & Charles Murray, *The Bell Curve: Intelligence and Class Structure in American Life* (New York: Free Press, 1994), 562.

21. Ibid., 562.

22. Ibid., 418.

23. Ibid., 441.

24. Murray N. Rothbard, *Man, Economy, and State: A Treatise of Economic Principles* (Los Angeles: Nash, 1970).

25. See Peter Boettke, "Friedrich A. Hayek (1899–1992)," Department of Economics, New York University. Available: www.econ.nyu.edu/user/boettke/hayek.htm, p. 1. Unpublished manuscript.

26. Friedrich Hayek, *The Road to Serfdom* (Chicago: University of Chicago Press, 1994).

27. Milton Friedman, *Capital and Freedom* (Chicago: University of Chicago Press, 1962), 89.

28. Ibid., 92.

29. William Simon used the term *counterintelligentsia* in his book, *A Time for Truth* (New York: Readers Digest Press, 1978), 228.

30. James Smith, *The Idea Brokers and the Rise of the New Policy Elite* (New York: Free Press, 1991), 181.

31. Simon, *A Time for Truth*, 233.

32. Friedman, *Capital and Freedom*, xii.

33. Ibid.

34. Simon, *A Time for Truth* 232–233.

35. Ibid., 230.

36. Smith, *The Idea Brokers*, 182.

37. David M. Ricci, *The Transformation of American Politics: The New Washington and the Rise of Think Tanks* (New Haven, CT: Yale University Press, 1993), 166.

38. Murray N. Rothbard, "Historical Origins," in *The Twelve-Year Sentence: Radical Views of Compulsory Schooling*, ed. William F. Rickenbacker (New York: Dell, 1974), 29.

39. Ibid., 2.

40. Joel Spring, *Wheels in the Head: Educational Philosophies of Authority, Freedom, and Culture From Socrates to Paulo Freire* (New York: McGraw-Hill, 1994). Despite its translation into five languages, I never received a penny for this book until, after getting back the copyright in the 1990s, I added sections and published it as a textbook through McGraw-Hill.

41. John Coons, William H. Clune, & Stephan Sugarman, *Private Wealth and Public Education* (Cambridge, MA: Harvard University Press, 1970).

42. David Boaz, "The Public School Monopoly: America's Berlin Wall," in *Liberating Schools: Education in the Inner City* (Washington, DC: Cato Institute, 1991), 1–25.

43. Libertarian Party 1996 National Campaign Platform. Available: http://www.ag.uius.edu:8001/liberty/libweb.html, 1.

44. Ibid., 7–8.

45. Smith, *The Idea Brokers*, 154–159.

46. A list of the board of trustees and biographical sketches of the staff can be found on the Hudson Institute's home page, http://www.al.com/hudson/. Funding information can be found on the House Democrat Research World Wide Web page, http://www.house.gov/democrats/research/.

47. Ibid.

48. Heritage Foundation, *The Insider*. Available: http://www.heritage.org/heritage/resource_bank/oct_insider.html.

49. Hudson Institute Web site: http://www.al.com/hudson/.

50. See biographical sketch in Louis V. Gerstner, Jr., with Roger Semerand, Denis Philip Doyle, & William B. Johnston, *Reinventing Education: Enterpreneurship in America's Public Schools* (New York: Dutton, 1994), 275–276.

51. Ibid., 10.

52. See http://www.edexcellence.net.

53. Ibid.

54. Ibid.

55. Hudson Institute Web site: http://www.al.com/hudson/.

56. Chester Finn, Jr., "Beating Up on Charter Schools," *The New York Times*, 24 August 1996, A23.

57. "Chester E. Finn, Jr. Biographical Summary." Available: http://www.edexcellence.net.

58. "Diane Ravitch Biographical Summary." Available: http://www.edexcellence.net.

59. See http://www.nynetworks.org/home.

60. Biographical summaries of Chester Finn, Jr. and Diane Ravitch can be found at http://www.edexcellence.net.

61. Chester Finn, Jr., "Education Without the State 7/10/96." Available: http://www.edexcellence.net.

62. See Diane Ravitch, *The Troubled Crusade: American Education 1945–1980* (New York: Basic Books, 1983).

63. Chester Finn, Jr., & Diane Ravitch, "Educational Reform 1995–96. Part III: Reinventing Education." Available: http://www.edexcellence.net, 2.

64. Chester Finn, Jr., & Dian Ravitch, "Educational Reform 1995–96. Part V: Reforming the Federal Role." Available: http://www.edexcellence.net, 2.

65. Ibid., 6.

66. Ibid., 7.

67. Ibid., 7.

68. Ibid., 10.

69. Jonathan Kozol, *Savage Inequalities: Children in America's Schools* (New York: Crown, 1991).

70. Jacques Steinberg, "Enrollment Surge in New York City Strains Schools," *New York Times*, 29 August 1996, 1; Rachel L. Swarns, "A Bronx School Asks: 'Just Where Will We All Sit?'," *New York Times*, 30 August 1996, B1.

71. For a history of this debate, see Larry Cuban, *How Teachers Taught: Constancy and Change in American Classrooms, 1890–1980* (White Plains, NY: Longman, 1984).

72. Lind, *Up From Conservatism*, 199.

73. David C. Berliner & Bruce Biddle, *The Manufactured Crisis: Myths, Fraud, and the Attack on America's Public Schools* (New York: Addison-Wesley, 1995).

74. Chester E. Finn & Diane Ravitch, "Magna Charter? A Report Card on School Reform in 1995," *Policy Review* (fall 1995): 74; Dinesh D'Souza, "We the Slaveowners: In Jefferson's America, Were Some Men Not Created Equal?", *Policy Review* (fall 1995): 74.

75. D'Souza, "We the Slaveowners," 21.

76. Dinesh D'Souza, *Illiberal Education: The Politics of Race and Sex on Campus* (New York: Vintage Books, 1992); Dinesh D'Souza, *The End of Racism* (New York: Free Press, 1995).

77. Ibid., 42.

78. Smith, *The Idea Brokers*, 197.

79. Ibid., 197–202.

80. Allyson Tucker, *A Special Report to the Appropriations Committees, Candidates for Rescission in the FY 1995 Education Budget*. The Heritage Foundation, Committee Brief No. 7, 24 February 1995, 4.

81. Quoted in Smith, *The Idea Brokers*, 178.

82. Peter Brimelow, *Alien Nation: Common Sense About America's Immigration Disaster* (New York: HarperPerennial, 1996), 278.

83. Ibid.

84. Ibid., 301–305.

85. Ibid., 264.

86. Ibid., 264–265.

87. Quoted in Smith, *The Idea Brokers*, 20.

Chapter 3

The Neoconservative Republican Agenda: Testing, Privatization, and Charters

◆ ◆ ◆

Banging and stomping their feet, students from Houston's Knowledge Is Power Program (KIPP) school were seated in a mock classroom on stage at the 2000 Republican national convention chanting multiplication tables and rapped, "Read, baby, read."[1] The trademark chant of the KIPP schools echoed through the convention hall, "Knowledge is power, power is freedom, and I want it."[2] This was the same KIPP school applauded by the Manhattan Institute's Chester E. Finn, Jr., and whose effort to franchise received support from the owners of Gap Jeans. Used to highlight George W. Bush's educational platform, the KIPP school represented the Republican dream of privatization of education and parental choice.

However, Bush abandoned the recent Republican objections to federal involvement in education. His advocacy of using federal funds and federal pressure to support a program that combined vouchers with state testing was in conflict with the religious right's opposition to federal involvement in education. How could this change be justified? As usual, Finn was asked for his opinion by the *New York Times*. Finn's response was "Bush believes that his experience reforming education in Texas can be refracted on the whole country. In his view, the federal government is sort of like a magnifying glass—It takes energy originating elsewhere and focuses it and concentrates it."[3]

Perhaps Bush's membership in the religious right and his advocacy of faith-based organizations for social programs assured members of the Christian Coalition that federal power would not conflict with religious values. In fact, the education section of the 2000 national Republican platform reiterated the concept of compassionate conservatism: "We approach [education] with compassionate conservatism, a concept that is as old as the pioneers heading West."[4] Traditionally, the last thing the religious right wants is a curriculum controlled by national or state academic standards. Although members of the religious right support choice, they do not support government control of what is taught to their children. The Christian Coalition's influence on the 1996 Republican party platform resulted in approval of school choice and a harshly worded condemnation of federal involvement in education. The 1996 platform stated that "Our formula is as simple as it is sweeping: The federal government has no constitutional authority to be involved in school curricula or to control jobs in the work place."[5]

During the 1996 campaign, Republican candidate Bob Dole, raising clasping hands with televangelist Pat Robertson over a podium marked "Christian Coalition," pledged support of school vouchers and school prayer. Robertson warn you: "Remember, the Christian Coalition are hard-core activists ... [and they want you to go after the vote of] people who are identified as born-again, or evangelical church members, or conservative Roman Catholics."[6]

Given the conditions of the 1996 campaign, one of Bush's great accomplishments was to bridge the gap between the religious right and the neoconservative factions of the Republican party. The *New York Times's* Robin Toner reported from the 2000 Republican convention:

> Republicans finished work today on a platform that embraces much of Gov. George W. Bush's educational agenda, over the objections of some conservatives who warned that the party was breaking with the get-the-government-off-our-backs philosophy of the Reagan revolution. But conservatives held sway on an array of social issues, from gays in the military to contraceptive counseling in school-based clinics. The 107-member platform committee voted against a call to abolish the Department of Education, and in favor of Mr. Bush's education principles which conservatives had resisted in early subcommittee action. Bush allies termed both votes a major victory, emblematic of their candidate's efforts to create a new Republican Party with more appeal to the voters in the center.[7]

NEOCONSERVATIVES, BUSINESS, AND NATIONAL STANDARDS

Bush's educational triumph at the 2000 Republican convention can be traced back to the 1983 report *A Nation at Risk*. After founding the Education Excellence Network in 1981, Finn and Diane Ravitch recalled that their efforts received little public attention until the appearance of *A Nation at Risk*. "To put it mildly," they remembered, "this bombshell [*A Nation at Risk*] awakened parents, educators, governors, legislators, and the press .... Its warning of 'a rising tide of mediocrity' helped launch what came to be called the excellence movement, which included a mass of other commissions, studies, and reports."[8]

Issued by the Reagan administration, *A Nation at Risk* contains the unproven and often-repeated claim that the poor quality of schools was responsible for the difficulties U.S. corporations were experiencing competing in international markets. The report opened with alarming language: "Our nation is at risk. Our once unchallenged preeminence in commerce, industry, science and technological innovation is being overtaken by competitors throughout the world." Dramatically claiming that the poor quality of U.S. schools threatened the future of the nation, the report stated: "If an unfriendly foreign power had attempted to impose on America the mediocre educational performance that exists today, we might well have viewed it as an act of war."[9]

The traditional Republican approach to educational policies is to link economic performance with the quality of public schools. In this tradition, the primary role of the schools is to educate workers—called *human capital*—who will improve economic efficiency and technological development. During the 1950s, the National Manpower Council played a major role in defining the human capital policies of the Republican party. Founded in 1951 in response to the labor needs of the Cold War, the National Manpower Council, reflecting the technological needs of the Cold War, recommended in its first report in 1951 that Selective Service deferments should be used "to insure a continuous supply of college-trained people whose general education and specialized knowledge are essential to the nation's civilian and military strength."[10] In 1953, the council issued *A Policy for Scientific and Professional Manpower*, warning that the Soviet Union's totalitarian methods were forcing large numbers of students to study science and engineering, which would make the Soviet Union superior in technology and military weaponry. The problem facing the United States was persuading more talented youth to enter technological fields.[11]

The Soviet launching of Sputnik in 1957 seemed to confirm the warnings of the National Manpower Council. Within a month of the Sputnik launch, President Eisenhower called on the U.S. school system to educate more scientists and engineers to match the large numbers being graduated by the Soviet educational system. "My scientific advisers," Eisenhower declared, "place [the shortage of scientists and engineers] above all other immediate tasks of producing missiles, of developing new techniques in the armed services."[12] Convinced that the education of more scientists and engineers was the key to winning the Cold War, Eisenhower proposed the National Defense Education Act, which was passed by Congress in 1958. It is ironic that when one considers later Republican objections to federal involvement in education, the National Defense Education Act—with its scholarships, student loans, support for the development of new math and science curricula for public schools, and aid for recruiting more teachers—actually was one of the first major involvements in modern times of the federal government in public education.

Republican concerns with human capital development continued into the 1970s, when President Richard Nixon supported federal grants for career education programs. Nixon hoped that career education would create a closer alignment of the public school curriculum with the needs of the labor market. Within this framework, public schools would convince students to think about education in relation to a future job; to focus their learning on the skills required for that job; and then, after graduation, to move smoothly into the labor market.[13]

Therefore, A Nation at Risk was not a sharp break from previous Republican considerations of schooling as an important part of economic planning. The emphasis on school improvement as a means of strengthening the position of U.S. corporations in world markets continued in later reports. A Nation Prepared: Teachers for the 21st Century (1986), issued by the Carnegie Forum on Education and the Economy, blamed economic conditions on the low quality of American teachers who were preparing workers for the new global economy. A Nation Prepared proposed a redirection for American schools from preparation for mass-production industries to preparation for knowledge-based industries.[14]

The report urged schools to replace the repetitive learning methods needed for mass production with learning methods that develop higher order thinking. According to the report, these older instructional methods could be packaged easily in textbooks that provided instructional guides for teachers. In the new world economy, the report claimed, the development of higher order thinking requires workers who are prepared for nonroutine and unexpected tasks. For the writers of A Nation Prepared, meeting the needs of the world economy required the abandonment of traditional methods of instruction, school organization, and teacher training.

Although A Nation Prepared anticipated later demands by neoconservatives and New Democrats to create "break the mold" of schools, Action for Excellence (1983) drew governors and corporate leaders into the snowballing school reform movement. *Action for Excellence* was issued by the Education Commission of the States' Task Force on Education for Economic Growth, which was composed of representatives of major corporations and governors. Its funding came from some of the largest corporations, including IBM and Xerox, whose chief executives—Louis V. Gerstner, Jr., and David Kearns—later worked with neoconservatives on school reform. The involvement of governors demonstrated the political grip of school reform. By 1989, neoconservative Gov. Lamar Alexander and New Democrat Gov. Bill Clinton were working for school reform.

Involvement of business in public school reform highlights a major difference between adherents of Austrian economics and neoconservatives. To advocates of free markets there are major dangers in corporations using government to protect their place in the market. Austrian economists worry as much about business control of government, which is fascism, as they do about bureaucratic control of the marketplace. In contrast, neoconservatives accept business involvement in government along with the government's role in exercising moral and social authority. The increasing role of business is indicated by a statement in *Action for Excellence*: "If the business community gets more involved in both the design and delivery of education, we are going to become more competitive as an economy."[15]

In 1994, Gerstner, CEO and chairman of IBM, explained that he "wanted to go beyond traditional business partnerships that enhance schools by providing equipment, mentors, or increased opportunities .... While these generous efforts may brighten the picture for a few children, they do not change 'the system.' "[16] Claiming that his interest in educational reform "is fueled by intense anger, and frustration," Gerstner emphatically asserted that "You know that most young applicants are not qualified to do today's more intellectually demanding jobs, let alone tomorrow's."[17]

Neoconservatives are not alone in supporting business involvement in public schools. In 1996, President Bill Clinton welcomed 49 corporate chiefs and 40 governors to a national education summit held at IBM's conference center at Palisades, New York. Cohosting the event were Gerstner and Republican gov. Tommy Thompson. Both neoconservatives and New Democrats welcomed the summit meeting's emphasis on creating national and state academic standards.[18]

Two basic themes emerged from the interplay among neoconservatives, business people, and New Democrats. One was that low academic standards were resulting in poorly prepared students and inadequately trained teachers. The correction of these problems, it was argued, could be achieved through increased academic requirements for students and the certification of teachers. In addition, student achievement could be improved by requiring statewide or national achievement tests for promotion between grades and graduation. The same concept was applied to teachers. The result was that the late 1980s and early 1990s became a heyday for the creation of statewide student and teacher tests. The proposals contained in A *Nation Prepared* eventually resulted in the creation of the National Board for Professional Teaching Standards, which developed a national teacher's examination and began awarding national teacher certification in 1993.[19]

The second theme was that public schools needed to be redesigned to meet the needs of the "Information Age." Advocates of school choice could now claim that competition would produce new types of schools. In addition, the concern with redesigning schools provided a rationale for charter and for-profit schools.

GOALS 2000

George W. Bush's father, President George Bush, favored strong federal involvement in education. In this respect, George W. is carrying on his father's tradition with the major difference being George W.'s closer affiliation with the religious right. His father's commitment to federal involvement in education is exemplified by Goals 2000, which also highlights the criss-crossing lines between the educational policies of neoconservatives and Al Gore and Clinton's New Democrats. President George Bush officially inaugurated Goals 2000 at the President's Education Summit With Governors at the University of Virginia on September 27, 1989. The governors were formally represented by the National Governors' Association, which was chaired by Republican Governor, and later Secretary of Education, Lamar Alexander. The vice chairman was Gov. Clinton.

Emphasizing the themes of human capital, academic standards, and reinvention of schools, the joint statement issued in 1989 by the President and the National Governors' Association reiterated what was becoming an unquestioned assumption: "As a nation we must have an educated work force, second to none, in order to succeed in an increasingly competitive world economy."[20] Linking human capital to national academic standards, the joint statement declared: "We believe that the time has come, for the first time in U.S. history, to establish clear national performance goals, goals that will make us internationally competitive."[21]

A revolution, according to this Bush administration, would take place with the implementation of Goals 2000, which remained amazingly consistent as it traveled from the Republican Bush administration to the Clinton administration. Laced with references to "productive employment," "first in the world in science and mathematics," and "global economy," the goals and the strategy for the implementation of Goals 2000 promised a new day for American schools:

America's Education Goals By the Year 2000

1. All children in America will start school ready to learn.
2. The high school graduation rate will increase to at least 90%.
3. American students will leave grades 4, 8, and 12 having demonstrated competency in challenging subject matter including English, mathematics, science, history, and geography, and every school in America will ensure that all students learn to use their minds well, so they may be prepared for responsible citizenship, further learning, and productive employment in our modern economy.
4. U.S. students will be first in the world in science and mathematics achievement.
5. Every adult American will be literate and will possess the knowledge and skills necessary to compete in a global economy and exercise the rights and responsibilities of citizenship.
6. Every school in America will be free of drugs and violence and will offer a disciplined environment conducive to learning.[22]

Goal 3 sets the stage for George W. Bush's later advocacy of pressuring states to administer tests to measure student competency.

To help implement Goals 2000, President Bush appointed Lamar Alexander as Secretary of Education in 1991 and the ever-present Ravitch as Assistant Secretary of Education in charge of the Office of Educational Research and Improvement. Alexander had built his political career in Tennessee with the promise that educational reform would improve the state's economy. In 1996, Alexander was a candidate for the Republican Presidential nomination.

With claims that education was the key to the economic success of the United States, President Bush, with the aid of Alexander and Ravitch, released on April 18, 1991, a plan for implementing Goals 2000: *America*

2000: An Education Strategy. Without any proof that the school quality was the cause of U.S. problems in international trade or that school reform would improve the economy, Bush, using the language of human capital, stated:

> Down through history, we've defined resources as soil and stone, land and the riches buried beneath. No more. Our greatest national resource lies within ourselves ... the capacity of the human mind .... If we want to keep America competitive in the coming century, ... we must accept responsibility for educating everyone among us.[23]

Speaking to the concerns of corporate leaders who did not want school reform to cost a bundle, and to neoconservatives who believed the public school monopoly and bureaucracy were the problem, and not money, Bush claimed that a 33% increase in educational spending since 1981 had not resulted in a 33% improvement in schools' performance. "Dollar bills don't educate students," Bush asserted. "To those who want to see real improvement in American education, I say: There will be no renaissance without revolution."[24]

The heart of the implementation strategy was an "Accountability Package," which, according to its introductory statement, served all six goals. The first step in the accountability package, and dear to the hearts of neoconservatives, was the creation of world-class standards by a national education goals panel that would "incorporate both knowledge and skills, to ensure that, when they leave school, young Americans are prepared for further study and the work force."[25] The second step was writing American achievement tests based on the world-class standards created by the national education goals panel. These voluntary tests were "to foster good teaching and learning as well as to monitor student progress."[26] Disappointing both the religious right and neoconservatives, Bush proposed that school choice be limited to public schools. Bush's son would later extend the school choice option to include private schools.

The major components of George Bush's educational strategies were national academic standards, national achievement tests, and corporate involvement in American schools. All of these proposals were made in the context of improving the competitive edge of American corporations in international markets. As David Hornbeck, former Maryland state superintendent, commented at the time, "For the first time in American history, what is good for kids and what is good for business coincides almost on a one-for-one basis."[27]

STANDARDS AND TESTS: THE POLITICS
OF CULTURE

It is surprising that no one seemed to give much thought to the ideological problems of creating standards and tests. Even in mathematics, a field often thought of as politically neutral, there exist major differences over what should be taught and how it should be taught. When the "New Math," as it was called in the early 1960s, was introduced, its emphasis on teaching arithmetic to elementary school children using set and number theories encountered a storm of protest from conservative parents who wanted arithmetic instruction to use traditional methods, such as memorization of the multiplication table.[28]

In the development of national standards and tests in the 1990s, history has proved to be the most politically contentious subject. Because history is shaped by and contains political values, the debate over history standards reflects broad divisions in political ideas. In 1986, foreshadowing the national standards debate over history, California Superintendent of Public Instruction Bill Honig appointed Ravitch, who at the time was an adjunct professor at Teachers College of Columbia University, and Charlotte Crabtree, a professor of education at the University of California, Los Angeles, to a panel to rewrite the state social studies curriculum. In 1987, California officials approved a framework for the teaching of history that was primarily written by Ravitch and Crabtree.[29]

The controversy over the California framework centered on its portrayal of the United States as a land of immigrants sharing a common set of values. The debate occurred in New York, with Arthur Schlesinger, Jr., and Ravitch playing a major role.[30] The dispute highlights significant differences regarding the teaching and interpretation of U.S. history. For neoconservatives, the major purpose of teaching history is to create national unity by teaching a common set of political and social values. These common values, according to the neoconservative approach, should be based on the beliefs underlying American institutions. In Schlesinger's words, "For better or worse, the White Anglo-Saxon Protestant tradition was for two centuries—and in crucial respects still is—the dominant influence on American culture and society .... The language of the new nation, its laws, its institutions, its political ideas, its literature, its customs, its precepts, its prayers, primarily derived from Britain."[31] Using similar words, Honig stated that "This country has been able to celebrate pluralism but keep some sense of the collective that holds us together .... Democracy has certain core ideas—freedom of speech, law, procedural rights, the way we deal with each other."[32]

From the conservative perspective, the teaching of core values would help reduce racial and ethnic strife in U.S. society and ensure the perpetuation of traditional American values. Within this framework the content of U.S. history would emphasize the common struggles and benefits received from U.S. institutions by the diverse cultural groups composing its population. The study of differing cultures in the United States, such as Native American and African, should emphasize tolerance and unity under common institutions. Similar to Dinesh D'Souza's interpretation of slavery discussed in chapter 2, slavery is presented as a negative institution that developed in an otherwise positive society which, in the end, provided a better life for the descendants of enslaved Africans.

The major objections to the neoconservative interpretation of U.S. history come from individuals who practice the politics of cultural identity. As I discuss in chapter 5, the politics of cultural identity splintered the left in the United States and made it difficult to formulate a coherent left-wing ideology.

One objection to the California framework came from Nathan Huggins, a Harvard professor of African American studies and history. Huggins warned, "A stress on 'common culture' turns history into a tool of national unity, mandated principally by those anxious about national order and coherence."[33] There was outrage among some African Americans, Mexican Americans, and Native Americans at the concept of the United States being a land of immigrants. All three groups could claim to be unwilling members of U.S. society that had been forced into participation by slavery and conquest. From this perspective, the history of the United States is marked by White violence against Africans, Mexicans, Asians, and Native Americans. This racial violence brings into question the worth of White Anglo-Saxon values undergirding American institutions.

Stanford University professor of African and Afro-American studies Sylvia Wynter argued that the California history framework "does not move outside the conceptual field of our present essentially Euro-American cultural model." The framework, she argued, did not provide a means for understanding the plight of minority groups in the United States. Wynter asked:

How did the dispossession of the indigenous peoples, their subordination, and the mass enslavement of the people of Black African descent come to seem "just and virtuous" actions to those who affected them? How does the continuance of this initial dispossession, in the jobless, alcohol-ridden reservations, the jobless drug and crime ridden inner cities ... still come to seem to all of us, as just, or at the very least, to be in the nature of things?[34]

Joyce King, then a professor of education at Santa Clara University and one of the leading critics of the California framework, was particularly disturbed by the "we are all immigrants" interpretation of U.S. history. King called this approach a "dysconscious racism ... an impaired consciousness or a distorted way of thinking about race ... [that] tacitly accepts dominant White norms and privileges."[35] The California framework, she argued, presents a triumphant chronological history, which recognizes the unfortunate conquest of Indians and enslavement of Africans, progressing to an inevitable point when all groups are able to acquire the supposed "superior" values of White Anglo-Saxon society. In this context, national unity requires that all cultural groups recognize the advantages of White Anglo-Saxon traditions.

The California controversy foreshadowed later discussions about the politics of knowledge. After Ravitch's appointment in 1991 as Assistant Secretary of Education in charge of the Office of Educational Research and Improvement, Charlotte Crabtree's National Center for History in Schools received a joint award of $1.6 million from Ravitch's office and the National Endowment of the Humanities to develop national history standards. At the time, the National Endowment for the Humanities was headed by Lynne Cheney, who shared a common philosophy about the humanities with her predecessor, William Bennett.

To the horror of Ravitch and Cheney, the first set of national standards in history contained teaching examples that, in Cheney's words, "make it sound as if everything in America is wrong and grim." Cheney complained that the teaching examples contained 17 references to the Ku Klux Klan and 19 references to McCarthyism, whereas there was no mention of Paul Revere, Thomas Edison, and other "politically incorrect White males."[36] The teaching examples were done outside the neoconservative political fold by Carol Gluck, a professor of history at Columbia University. Using what she called a democratic process, Gluck spent 2 years meeting with more than 6,000 parents, teachers, businesspeople, and school administrators.[37] Outraged, Cheney founded a Washington-based Committee to Review National Standards to apply political pressure for a revision of the history standards.

In 1995, the National Center for History in the Schools announced that it was revising the history standards and teaching examples. Claiming a victory, Ravitch said she hoped that "we can declare this particular battlefront in the culture wars to be ended."[38] In reporting Ravitch's statement, Karen Diegmueller explained that Ravitch was "a panelist who not only had criticized the documents but had commissioned their creation when she served as an assistant secretary in the U.S.

Department of Education."[39] Diegmueller reported that the criticisms of the history standards were primarily from neoconservatives who contended, in Diegmueller's words, that "the standards undercut the great figures that traditionally have dominated the landscape of history and portray the United States and the West as oppressive regimes that have victimized women, minorities, and third-world countries."[40] What the critics wanted, Diegmueller wrote, was a history that emphasized U.S. accomplishments and provided students with uplifting ideals.

With a cynical tone, Diegmueller opened a later *Education Week* article with these words: "Timbuktu has disappeared. Pearl Harbor has ascended. George Washington is in; Eleanor Roosevelt is out. And names and places like Joseph McCarthy and Seneca Falls, N.Y., whose prominence irked critics ... have been allotted one mention apiece."[41] She also reported an attempt to give a more upbeat tone to the introductions to the 10 eras of U.S. history delimited by the standards.

In their 1996 campaign book, Bob Dole and Jack Kemp joined the chorus demanding that a more upbeat history be taught in public schools. Among three failures of public schools, Dole and Kemp identified this: "Where schools should instill an appreciation of our country and its history, often they seem to reflect a blindness toward America and its finer moments."[42]

The culture wars surrounding the history standards mirrored broad differences in political values between neoconservatives and the left. What is important to note is that these differences went beyond the usual concept of politics to include issues of knowledge. The politics of knowledge involve questions such: Who should determine the political values taught to students? What political values should be taught to students? What is the relation between the political beliefs of politicians and the political ideas presented to students? The neoconservative criticism of the history standards underscores the general attempt by right-wing think tanks to influence the minds of citizens.

FOR-PROFIT AND CHARTER SCHOOLS

Educational entrepreneur Chris Whittle came up with the idea of franchising for-profit schools. Whittle's plans fit nicely into Austrian economics: Within a free market, for-profit schools would compete for students. However, in this case Whittle was betting on a government voucher system that would allow parents to choose between private and public schools. Whittle wanted to capture some of this voucher money by designing a conservative and technologically advanced school that could be franchised across the country.

Politically speaking, Whittle is on the right. He made his position in the culture wars evident when he convinced the Federal Express Corporation to help fund the publication of Schlesinger's attack on multicultural education, *The Disuniting of America*.[43] Schlesinger's book carries the imprint of Whittle Direct Books and has full-page ads for Federal Express scattered through the text. Reminiscent of William Simon, Whittle tried to ensure that Schlesinger's educational ideas received a wide audience by sending free copies to business leaders around the country.

Whittle's political views are exemplified by his selection of the conservative president of Yale University, Benno Schmidt, to head his for-profit school enterprise. Whittle made the decision to hire Schmidt over food and drinks at a party in the ultraexclusive Hamptons on Long Island. Offered an annual salary of about $1 million, Schmidt left Yale in 1992 to head what was called the *Edison Project*. As one of the consultants on the project, Whittle hired Finn of the Hudson and Manhattan Institutes.[44]

Part of Whittle's plans went awry when the 1992 election of President Clinton seemed to doom any chance of government-financed public–private school vouchers. In addition, Whittle faced money problems that eventually led to his withdrawal from the project. At this point, the Edison Project moved from Whittle's home base in Knoxville, Tennessee, to its present location in New York City.[45]

Without public–private school vouchers, the only hope for the Edison Project was to franchise private schools that were dependent on tuition income or to seek some other form of public support. The opportunity for public support came, according to *New York* magazine reporter James Traub, when "governors William Weld of Massachusetts and Buddy Roemer of Colorado contacted Schmidt in the fall of 1992 that they would like to find a way to bring Edison into the public schools in their states. Both states went on to pass 'charter school' laws that permit states and school systems to award contracts to … private contractors."[46] With charter schools, the operation of for-profit schools is a possibility.

For many neoconservatives and individuals on the religious right, charter schools are a method for getting around the power of the educational bureaucracy. At the Hudson Institute, Finn, with support from the Pew Charitable Trusts, is conducting a major national study of charter schools. In an initial report in 1996, Finn, along with his colleagues Bruno Manno and Louann Bierlein, praised charter schools because "they serve the public in a different way, more like the voluntary institutions of 'civil society' than the compulsory/monopolistic organs of government."[47] For the religious right, charter schools provide a possible source of public funding of schools established on their values. Consequently, the 1996 Republican platform included charter schools in its list of methods to initiate school choice, stating that "we support and vigorously work for mechanisms, such as opportunity scholarships, block grants, school rebates, charter schools, and vouchers, to make parental choice in education a reality for all parents."[48]

The first charter school law, enacted in Minnesota in 1991, allows anyone to present a school plan to the state board of education. If the plan is approved by the state board, a charter is granted to allow the operation of the school at public expense. By 1996, 25 states and the District of Columbia had charter school laws with differing provisions stating what groups or individuals could initiate charter plans, who had power of approval, and the required degree of compliance with state regulations. Finn's national survey of charter schools found that "some state laws are more generous in bestowing the charter designation than in actually liberating schools to make key decisions ... [and that] some ... charter schools ... remain subordinate to district administrations and school boards."[49]

In Massachusetts, considered by Finn's report as having the strongest charter school law, one fifth of the state's 25 charter schools in 1996 were for-profit schools. Two of the for-profit schools were operated by the Edison Project, two by Sabis International, and one by Alternative Public Schools. Finn's report praised the Massachusetts charter system's for-profit schools and the provisions allowing charter schools the freedom to use uncertified teachers and to ignore all teachers' collective bargaining agreements by unions. These last provisions are strongly opposed by the teachers' unions.

At its 1996 convention, the American Federation of Teachers issued a report demanding that collective-bargaining agreements cover charter schools and that charter schools be required to hire certified teachers. In an op-ed article in the *New York Times*, Finn accused the teachers' unions of trying to cripple the charter school movement to protect their own interests. Reflecting the antieducational establishment bias of neoconservatives, Finn lauded charter schools: "By eroding the monopoly of unions, charter schools threaten their control. By offering a popular alternative to regular schools, they call attention to how poorly the status quo serves many students."[50]

Members of the religious right and neoconservatives support charter schools because they provide educational alternatives for parents and children, sidestep the educational establishment, and allow for a free market for the operation of for-profit schools. New Democrats, as I discuss in chapter 4, support charter schools under the rubric of "reinventing the school." The 2000 Democratic candidate Al Gore's and former President Clinton's concept of charter schools was influenced by the strong political support they received from the two teachers' unions.

REPUBLICAN AGENDA FOR THE 21ST CENTURY

President George W. Bush's administration has continued the neoconservative agenda of testing and vouchers. The problem Bush faces is balancing the Republican commitment to local control with federal involvement in education. Bush tried to address this issue by calling for federal requirements to force states to prepare and administer statewide testing programs. In this manner, he could argue that there was no federal intrusion in local education through a national testing program. The 2000 Republican platform emphasized this balance between local and state power: "We endorse the principles of Governor Bush's education reforms, which will: Raise academic standards through increased local control and accountability to parents."[51]

Taking a cue from George W.'s brother Gov. Jeb Bush's Florida plan, which allows parents of children in failing schools to use vouchers to select private schools, the 2000 Republican platform asserted that it would "assist states in closing the achievement gap and empower needy families to escape persistently failing schools by allowing federal dollars to follow their children to the school of their choice."[52] Vouchers, of course, according neoconservatives would enhance parental power in opposition to state and federal power. In this manner George W. Bush could argue that his federally mandated state testing programs would actually increase parental control.

Acting quickly after his inauguration, Bush sent to Congress his education plan, including a proposal for private-school choice. Bush's spokesman Ari Fleischer declared about the proposal, "President-elect Bush thinks this is going to be a powerful incentive to make sure that all our public schools live up to the standards that can and must be set for them."[53] The initial Bush plan called for more student testing, the punishing and rewarding of states depending on pupil performance, expanding public charter schools, and spending $5 billion on reading instruction and research. The plan also called for federal funds going to schools serving low-income students that failed to meet standards for 3 straight years be given to parents to be used either to transport students to another public school, private school vouchers, or tutoring. The controversial part of the plan was the proposal for private school vouchers. Regarding the voucher plan, Bush declared, "Parents and children who have only bad options must eventually get good options if we're to succeed all across the country."[54]

Also, as a nod to state control, Bush placed the responsibility for testing in the hands of state governments. States would "select and design assessments of their choosing" for students in Grades 3–8. Federal money would be used by states to develop the tests. The plan would require yearly administration of the tests and states to report each school the results "by race, gender, English language proficiency, disability and socioeconomic status."[55]

Buried in Bush's tax plan was a call for a scheme that dated back to the Reagan years, namely tax credits for tuition spent on private schools. This has been a plan dear to hearts of members of the religious right and neoconservatives. Bush proposed that parents be allowed to deduct up to $5,000 of their yearly income to pay the educational expenses of each of their children attending private elementary and secondary schools. This could mean a tax credit of $20,000 for parents with four children attending private schools. He also proposed the use of tax-deductible education savings accounts for paying private school expenses.[56] All of these proposals, except for the call for continued federal involvement in education, are consistent with Republican proposals dating from the 1980s and the Reagan administration.

CONCLUSION

One could argue that Bush's support of school choice, charter schools, for-profit schools, and national standards represents the achievement of William Simon's vision of creating a counterintelligentsia to fight the liberal establishment and to spread the Austrian economic dream, but do these elements of school reform actually conform to Simon's vision?

As articulated by Friedrich Hayek, the Austrian economic theory that influenced Simon criticizes business using government to accomplish its ends as severely as it does the collectivism of communism and socialism. Having experienced a world inhabited by totalitarian governments of the right and left, Hayek believed that the managed economy of the fascist state's alliance with business is as destructive of human freedom and economic vitality as the planned economy of socialist governments. From the perspective of Austrian economics, intellectual freedom can be attained only by severing all ties between government and schools.

Therefore, adhering to Austrian theory, neoconservatives are in the process of replacing the liberal establishment with a neoconservative establishment. Paralleling the symbiotic relationships among liberal intellectuals, liberal bureaucrats, and government programs, neoconservatives have created a network of intellectuals who justify their favorite government programs, receive government money and, in some cases, such as Finn and Ravitch, actually join the government bureaucracy.

Contrary to Austrian economic concerns, however, neoconservatives promote close links between business and government. A perfect example of fascist corporate planning is for-profit charter schools receiving government money. This symbiotic relationship portends a future nightmare of government favoritism, exploitation of students and teachers, and increasing educational costs. The results of for-profit charter schools could be far worse than anything that has happened in public schools.

Of course, neoconservatives do not want complete freedom for charter schools or any other type of school. Finn's report, discussed earlier, recommended "charter school accountability as a triad consisting of standards, assessments, and consequences." With a requirement to meet national or state academic standards and to be measured by federal or state tests, choice and charter schools simply become a method to enhance the learning of official government knowledge. There is no neoconservative allegiance to freedom of thought. As characterized by the struggle over the history standards, neoconservatives want their kind of knowledge to become the "official knowledge," as Michael Apple called it, of the public schools. In this context, Bush has seriously strayed from the original goals of Austrian economics.

NOTES

1. Jodi Wilogoren, "Analysis: For 2000, the G.O.P. Sees Education in a New Light," *New York Times on the Web*, 2 August 2000. Available: www.nytimes.com

2. Jodi Wilogoren, "Seeking to Clone Schools of Success for Poor," *New York Times on the Web*, 16 August 2000. Available: www.nytimes.com

3. Wilogoren, "Analysis: For 2000."

4. "Republican National Platform: Education and Opportunity: Leave No American Behind: A Responsibility Era." Available: http://www.rnc.org, 1.

5. "1996 Republican Platform." Available: http://www.rnnc.org, 21.

6. Gustav Niebuhr, "Dole Gets Christian Coalition's Trust and Prodding," *New York Times*, 16 September 1996, B8.

7. Robin Toner, "Bush's Stance on Education Prevails in Battle on Plank," *New York Times on the Web*, 29 July 2000. Available: www.nytimes.com

8. Chester Finn, Jr., & Diane Ravitch, "Educational Reform 1995–96 Introduction." Available: www.edexcellence.net, 2.

9. National Commission on Excellence in Education, *A Nation at Risk: The Imperatives for Educational Reform* (Washington, DC: Department of Education, 1983), 5.

10. National Manpower Council, *Student Deferment and National Manpower Policy* (New York: Columbia University Press, 1951), 8–9.

11. National Manpower Council, *A Policy for Scientific and Professional Manpower* (New York: Columbia University Press, 1953).

12. Dwight D. Eisenhower, "Our Future Security," in *Science and Education for National Defense: Hearings Before the Committee on Labor and Public Welfare, United States Senate, Eighty-Fifth Congress, Second Session* (Washington, DC: U.S. Government Printing Office, 1958), 1360.

13. See Joel Spring, *The Sorting Machine Revisited: National Educational Policy Since 1945*, rev. ed. (White Plains, NY: Longman, 1989), 151–155.

14. Task Force on Teaching as a Profession, *A Nation Prepared: Teachers for the 21st Century* (New York: Carnegie Corporation, 1986).

15. Task Force on Education for Economic Growth, *Action for Excellence* (Denver, CO: Education Commission of the States, 1983), 18.

16. Louis Gerstner, Jr., with Roger D. Semerad, Denis Philip Doyle, & William Johnston, *Reinventing Education: Entrepreneurship in America's Public Schools* (New York: Dutton, 1994), ix, italics added.

17. Ibid., pp. ix–x.

18. Millicent Lawton, "Summit Accord Calls for Focus on Standards," *Education Week*, 3 Apri 1996, 1, 14–15.

19. See Ann Bradley, "Pioneers in Professionalism," *Education Week*, 20 April 1993, 19–20, 24.

20. The President's Education Summit With Governors: Joint Statement, *America 2000: An Education Strategy* (Washington, DC: U.S. Government Printing Office, 1991), 73.

21. Ibid.

22. The President's Education Summit With Governors: Joint Statement, *America's Education Goals by the Year 2000* (Washington, DC: U.S. Government Printing Office), 19.

23. The President's Education Summit With Governors: Joint Statement, *Remarks by the President at the Presentation of the National Education Strategy* (Washington, DC: U.S. Government Printing Office), 1–2.

24. Ibid.

25. The President's Education Summit With Governors: Joint Statement, *For Today's Students: Better and More Accountable Schools* (Washington, DC: U.S. Government Printing Office), 21.

26. Ibid.

27. Jonathan Weisman, "Educators Watch With a Wary Eye as Business Gains Policy Muscle," *Education Week*, 31 July 1991, 25.

28. Spring, *The Sorting Machine*, 80–85.
29. Catherine Cornbleth & Dexter Waugh, *The Great Speckled Bird: Multicultural Politics and Education Policymaking* (Mahwah, NJ: Erlbaum, 1995), 16–17, 68–71.
30. Ibid., 93–185.
31. Arthur M. Schlesinger, Jr., *The Disuniting of America* (Knoxville, TN: Whittle Direct Books, 1991), 8.
32. Quoted in Caroline B. Cody, Arthur Woodward, & David L. Elliot, "Race, Ideology and the Battle Over the Curriculum," in *The New Politics of Race and Gender*, ed. Catherine Marshall (Washington, DC: Falmer Press, 1993), 55.
33. Quoted in Cornbleth & Waugh, *The Great Speckled Bird*, 85.
34. Quoted in Cornbleth & Waugh, *The Great Speckled Bird*, 65.
35. Quoted in Cornbleth & Waugh, *The Great Speckled Bird*, 66.
36. "Plan to Teach U.S. History Is Said to Slight White Males," *New York Times*, 26 October 1994, B12.
37. Carol Gluck, "Let the Debate Continue," *New York Times*, 26 October 1994, 23.
38. Karen Diegmueller, "Revise History Standards, Two Panels Advise," *Education Week*, 18 October 1995, 11.
39. Ibid.
40. Ibid.
41. Karen Diegmueller, "History Center Shares New Set of Standards," *Education Week*, 10 April 1996, 1.
42. Bob Dole & Jack Kemp, *Trusting the People* (New York: HarperCollins, 1996), 92.
43. Schlesinger, *The Disuniting of America*, 8.
44. James Traub, "Has Benno Schmidt Learned His Lesson?", *New York*, 31 October 1994, 51–59.
45. Ibid.
46. Ibid., 58.
47. Chester Finn, Jr., Bruno V. Manno, & Louann A. Bierlein, "Section 5: Conclusions and Recommendations," in *Charter Schools in Action: What Have We Learned?* (Indianapolis, IN: Hudson Institute, 1996), 5.
48. 1996 Republic Platform, 21.
49. Finn et al., "Introduction and Overview," in *Charter Schools in Acton: What Have We Learned?* (Indianapolis, IN: Hudson Institute, 1996), 4.
50. Chester Finn Jr., "Beating Up on Charter Schools," *New York Times* (24 August 1996), 23.
51. "Republican National Platform: Education and Opportunity," 2.
52. Ibid.
53. The Associated Press, "Bush to Send School Plant to Congress," *New York Times on the Web*, 21 January 2001. Available: www.nytimes.com
54. David Sanger, "Bush Pushes Ambitious Education Plan," *New York Times on the Web*, 24 January 2001. Available: www.nytimes.com
55. Ibid.
56. Diana Jean Schemo, "Focus on Tax Break as Support Wanes on School Vouchers," *New York Times on the Web*, 1 February 2001. Available: www.nytimes.com

Chapter 4

The New Democrats

◆ ◆ ◆

"It dismays me that some think-tank intellectuals," Secretary of Education Richard Riley cautioned in 1996, "are leading the retreat from the support of public education."[1] Referring to the denizens of right-wing institutes and foundations in his State of American Education Address, Riley warned, "I fear that they seek nothing less then the demise of public education."[2]

In contrast to Republican neoconservatives, the hallmark of the Bill Clinton–Al Gore administration was reinventing public education so that schools produced well-trained workers to meet the needs of businesses competing in the global economy. The 2000 Democratic platform declared, "We need to make sure Americans have the skills and tools they need to compete and win in the new knowledge-based, global economy."[3] Rejecting attempts to privatize education, Clinton and Gore put their faith in their ability to reform public schools. Gore stated during his 2000 Presidential campaign, "I think it's time to make revolutionary improvements in our public schools the No. 1 priority in the nation."[4]

The New Democratic movement of Clinton and Gore grew out of the work of the Democratic Leadership Council that Clinton chaired from 1991 to 1992. Formed in 1985 as an unofficial party organization, the council developed plans to move the Democratic party to the center of the political spectrum. The council quickly formed a think tank, the Progressive Policy Institute, to support scholars formulating the new centrist political position.[5]

The Democratic Leadership Council wanted to attract voters who crossed over to the Republican side during the backlash to antiwar dem-

onstrations, affirmative action, forced integration of schools, welfare policies, and cultural-identity politics. These fleeing White middle-class voters, the New Democrats argued, no longer believed the Democratic party
was working in their interests. In the 1960s and 1970s, according to New
Democrats, the New Deal coalition crumbled as southern and northern
working-class White voters concluded that the Democratic party represented the interests only of the poor, minority races, lesbians and gays,
and pacifists.

The cofounders of the Progressive Policy Institute, Will Marshall and
Robert Shapiro, were active in Democratic politics. Marshall worked for
many Democratic senators and representatives and served as a staff member of the House Subcommittee on Government Efficiency. At the time
of this writing, Marshall serves as both the project director of the Democratic Leadership Council and the president of the Progressive Policy Institute. While holding these positions, Marshall is a coeditor/author of
the New Democratic manifesto, *Mandate for Change*, which formed the
basic part of Clinton's 1992 political platform. Shapiro also worked in
Congress and now serves as a contributing editor to *The New Republic*.[6]

Concerned with winning back White middle-class voters, the New
Democrats eventually devised an educational platform that would give
the middle class federal aid to attend college and programs for upgrading
skills and finding new jobs. In addition, the New Democrats promised
that Goals 2000 would improve public schools and, because of these
better schools, graduates would get good jobs and become more competitive in the global labor market.

In 1990, the Progressive Policy Institute issued a strategy paper containing the ominous pronouncement: "It is time to say this: Our system of
public education is a bad system. It is terribly inequitable. It does not
meet the nation's needs and exploit's teachers' altruism. It hurts kids."[7]
Written by Ted Kolderie, a senior fellow of the Progressive Policy Institute, the policy paper advocated school choice and charter schools as solutions for the ills of public education. Kolderie argued that school choice
was not meaningful unless parents and students were presented with real
alternatives to the existing system. For Kolderie, this meant charter
schools. As an alternative to a choice plan based on vouchers, Kolderie
emphasized creating what he called "a new public school system" by allowing, "New schools ... [to] be formed by educators—administrators or
teachers—or by groups of parents. Other options include social-service
agencies or private groups in the learning business."[8]

In response to pressure from the teacher unions, Clinton later limited
Kolderie's proposal for charter schools to public school systems. Particu-

larly distasteful to the unions was Kolderie's suggestion that they allow for-profit learning businesses to charter schools. Therefore, accepting the often-stated opinion that public schools needed "reinvention" for the Information Age, the New Democrats supported public school choice and charter schools.

The New Democrats' educational program is based on the conviction that the plight of the modern worker in a global economy depends on rapidly changing job skills. This assumption resulted in an economic plan that leans heavily on education policies. For instance, consider the following problems and answers discussed by New Democrats:

1. Unemployment. The answer: educational opportunities to learn job skills needed in the new global economy.
2. Workers trapped in low-income and dead-end jobs. The answer: educational opportunities to improve job skills.
3. People who are unemployed because of restructuring and downsizing. The answer: educational opportunities to gain new job skills for the information and global economy.
4. Increasing inequality in income and wealth. The answer: expanded educational opportunities for the middle class and poor.
5. Improved overall economy. The answer: reinventing U.S. public schools for the Information Age and educating workers and students in the skills needed to help the United States expand in the global economy.
6. Students prepared for the new information world. The answer: wire all American schools for the Internet.

Future historians might consider the wiring of schools for the Internet as the most revolutionary educational program in the Clinton administration. During the 1996 campaign, Clinton and Gore met in Knoxville, Tennessee, to celebrate the world of cyberspace. At the gathering, Clinton prophesied, "The Internet will be the most profoundly revolutionary tool for educating our children in generations. I want to see the day when computers are as much a part of a classroom as blackboards, and we put the future at the fingertips of every American child."[9] To achieve this goal, he promised that if reelected he would make basic Internet access free to all schools and would spend $100 million to design high-speed fiberoptics and software for "a faster 'next generation' Internet."[10]

During the 2000 Presidential campaign Gore's agenda included that "every classroom and library [will be] wired to the Information Superhighway."[11] Also, the 2000 Democratic national platform declared the goal of "computer literacy for every child by the time they [*sic*] finish the eight [*sic*] grade."[12]

> We must launch a new crusade—calling on the resources of government, employers, the high-tech industry, community organizations, and unions— to move toward full Internet access in every home, for every family, all across the United States. We must not rest until Internet access is universal. We must also launch a new national effort to provide basic skills in the newest technology.[13]

There are two important and unproven assumptions to the New Democratic program. The first is that a skills mismatch between the worker and the labor market causes the basic problem of unemployment and dead-end jobs. Just give the worker the right skills, the New Democrats presume, and the problems are solved. This assumption, as I discuss, is currently being challenged.

The second assumption is that expanded educational opportunities will reduce the increasing inequality in income and wealth. This assumption is based on the relation between level of educational attainment and income. The problem in this assumption is educational inflation: As more people receive college degrees, the economic value of the college degree declines. In the context of educational inflation, the question is this: Can increased educational opportunities decrease economic inequalities?

CLINTON AND THE NEW DEMOCRATS

Clinton developed his political and educational agenda while serving as governor of Arkansas. After he lost the 1980 gubernatorial election, Hillary Clinton suggested that the next campaign should focus on education for economic revival. "Hillary Clinton," Meredith Oakley, the editor and political columnist of the *Arkansas-Democrat Gazette*, claimed, "was responsible for her husband's decision to emphasize education reform above all other matters."[14] This was 3 years before *A Nation at Risk* popularized the idea that educational reform was necessary to improve U.S. interests in global markets. During Clinton's successful 1982 gubernatorial election campaign he emphasized educational reform as the key to Arkansas's economic revival. Expansion of vocational and high-technology training programs, educational opportunity for the poor, and basic skills programs, Clinton claimed, would revitalize the state's economy.

After his second election, Clinton's campaign staff decided to create a public image of Clinton as the "education governor." The "education governor" image associated him with other southern governors using the same strategy. During the 1980s, Tennessee's Gov. Lamar Alexander—George Bush's future Secretary of Education—and South Carolina's Gov. Richard Riley—Clinton's future Secretary of Education—built their political careers on educational reform.

Hillary Clinton's role in designing Bill's educational image was extremely important. Beginning with her involvement as a lawyer in the Children's Defense Fund in the 1970s to the publication of her book, *It Takes A Village and Other Lessons Children Teach Us* (1996), she has influenced the educational agenda of the New Democrats. One of the significant reform strategies she and Bill agreed on was the use of government-created academic standards. After Bill won the gubernatorial election in 1982, he worked for the passage of Arkansas's Quality Education Act of 1983 and promptly appointed Hillary to chair the Education Standards Committee, whose members agree that its final report reflected Hillary's agenda.[15]

As the reader already knows, the conviction that tough educational standards could reform schools haunted educational politics throughout the 1990s. Hillary's Education Standards Committee proposed the testing of third-, sixth-, and eighth-grade students and Arkansas's teachers. Bill Clinton accepted the recommendations and announced that he would not raise taxes to give teachers a salary increase until state teachers took a basic skills test. "No test, no tax," he told the public.[16]

Clinton's education platform improved his public image and ratings in the polls.[17] His campaign strategists proclaimed that educational reform was a victory for the people and economy of Arkansas. In the public's mind, he was now the "education governor." With his popularity running high, Clinton spent little time campaigning in 1984. With the subsequent passage of legislation increasing the governor's term in office to 4 years, Clinton's position was secure.

Encouraged by the public image of "education governor," Clinton turned his attention to national politics. In 1986 he was elected vice chairperson of the National Governors Association. The chairperson of the organization was Lamar Alexander of Tennessee. In 1989, President Bush asked the National Governors' Association to develop what would become the Goals 2000 agenda.[18] Embodied in Goals 2000 were the principles of testing and educational standards that were the backbone of Clinton's political career as governor of Arkansas.

Chairing the Democratic Leadership Council in 1991 and 1992, Clinton applied the lessons he learned in Arkansas to developing a strategy to win voters back to the Democratic Party. In 1991, Clinton voiced the concerns of the Democratic Leadership Council:

> The working people and small-business people that used to vote for us don't anymore in a lot of tough elections because they have become convinced that the Democrats won't stand up for American interests abroad ... [and think we] will tax the middle class to give it to the poor with no strings attached.[19]

In 1992, the Democratic Leadership Council released programmatic guidelines in the form of *Mandate for Change*, for the New Democrats, who restated these New Democratic programs in the Clinton and Gore 1992 campaign book *Putting People First: How We Can All Change America*. With the same spirit as that of antigovernment Republicans, in *Putting People First* Clinton and Gore declared: "We must take away power from the entrenched bureaucracies and special interests that dominate Washington."[20] The anti-big government stance of the New Democrats appeared in the 1996 Democratic national platform: "The American people do not want big government solutions."[21]

By voicing an anti-big government attitude, New Democrats hope to distance themselves in the public mind from the frequently attacked image of liberals. *Liberalism* is now a politically sullied word because of the public relations campaign by right-wing think tanks. During the 1996 campaign, when Bob Dole accused Clinton of being a closet liberal, Clinton lashed back, citing a record of reducing the deficit, supporting the death penalty, banning assault weapons, and reforming welfare as proof of his New Democratic centrist politics.[22]

The New Democratic anti-big government stance is tempered by a belief that government still has the important role of ensuring the fair provision of services, such as health care and education. Hillary Clinton maintained that government needs to be trimmed but that it should not be made ineffectual in "fulfilling its basic responsibilities: (1) to build a strong, globally competitive economy that grows the middle class and shrinks the underclass; (2) to bring Americans together ... to fulfill their obligations to families, the environment, and those who need and deserve support."[23] Responding to radical antigovernment Austrian economists, Hillary Clinton warned that their rhetoric "argues against the excesses of government but not against excesses of the marketplace."[24] She wondered who would benefit from the elimination of government regulations controlling water pollution and whether the pursuit of profit in a free market would solve the problem.

Casting suspicion on proponents of marketplace economics and radical limitation of government activities, Hillary Clinton insisted that "this perspective exalts private initiative and regards those who exercise it as deserving to flourish virtually unencumbered by any mandate to share the wealth or apply it toward solving our common problems and creating common opportunities."[25]

In the 1996 campaign book *Between Hope and History*, Bill Clinton complained that the American political debate was divided between those arguing "for the government to spend more money on the same bureaucracies working in the same way" and those arguing "that government is inherently bad and all our problems would be solved if ... government [got] out of the way."[26] Clinton responded to these differences by indicating that between 1980 and 1992, when antigovernment attitudes dominated political rhetoric, the United States had the slowest job growth since the Depression, its national debt quadrupled, and society became more racially and ethnically divided. The "reinvented" government of the New Democrats will supposedly solve these problems.[27]

Consequently, New Democrats believe federal and state governments should "create a set of national standards for what students should know" while trusting the competition of the market to reinvent the school. In this context the federal government would act as a big sister or brother, helping states to carry out national mandates. For example, in *Putting People First*, Clinton and Gore argued that schools will be reformed by helping "states develop public school choice programs like those of Arkansas with protection from discrimination based on race, religion, or income."[28]

To attract middle-class voters, New Democrats shifted their focus from using education to help the poor achieve equality of opportunity to aiding middle-class families struggling to send their children to college. Rather than referring to the *war on poverty*, New Democrats use the term *lifetime learning*. The promise of lifetime learning is equal educational opportunity for all age groups and social classes. In *Putting People First* Clinton and Gore described their lifetime-learning strategy as investing "in our people at every stage of their lives."[29] They claimed that the strategy will put people first by dramatically improving the way parents prepare their children for school, giving students the chance to train for jobs or pay for college, and providing workers with the training and retraining they need to compete and win in tomorrow's economy.

Clinton's 1996 campaign promises dramatically illustrate the New Democrats' desire to extend government educational benefits to the middle class and to support lifetime learning. At the 1996 Democratic convention Clinton promised to "make two years of college just as universal … as a high school education is today."[30] To achieve this goal, he proposed a $1,500-a-year tuition tax credit that he described as "a hope scholarship for the first two years of college to make the typical community college education available to every American."[31] In addition, he called for a $10,000 income tax deduction for college tuition for working families and a $2,600 instructional grant to underemployed or unemployed workers for job training. In words highlighting the New Democrats' attempted appeal to the middle class, Clinton told convention delegates and television viewers, "We should not tax middle-income Americans for the money they spend on college. We'll get the money back down the road many times over."[32]

GOALS 2000 AND THE SKILLS-MISMATCH THEORY

In *Between Hope and History* Clinton echoed his Secretary of Labor Robert Reich's analysis of labor market problems: "There are people," Clinton observed, "principally the bottom half of America's hourly wage earners, who are working hard but aren't getting ahead because they don't have the kind of skills that are rewarded in this global economy."[33] Expressing concern about the splintering of the middle class as corporate restructuring forces many into the "anxious class" who must worry about debt and the next job, Hillary Clinton concluded that "midlevel managers and white-collar workers are increasingly vulnerable to becoming what Secretary of Labor Robert Reich calls 'frayed-collar workers in gold-plated times'."[34]

Appealing to the anxious class of middle- and working-class voters, the New Democrats offer broadened educational opportunities as solutions to the problems of declining real incomes, corporate restructuring and downsizing, and job insecurity. A fundamental premise of New Democrats—including the Clintons, Gore, and Reich—is that U.S. wages and jobs will not be protected from competition with the global labor market. Unlike laborers in the past, U.S. workers cannot feel secure in the knowledge that their wages are higher than those of workers in other countries doing comparable work. In the language of New Democrats, *competitive worker* refers to competition in a global market. Ultimately, this could mean a U.S. textile worker receiving the same wage as a textile worker in India or Honduras. In this context, if U.S. workers are going to achieve high salaries, then they must be trained for jobs that receive a high income in world labor markets.

Reich was the economic sage of the New Democrats. Important reasons for his influence are his 1991 book, *The Work of Nations: Preparing Ourselves for 21st-Century Capitalism*; his experience as an advisor in the Ford and Carter administrations, and his contributing editorship of *The New Republic*. Reich was a major influence on the Clinton administration's policies for education and human capital. He concluded that there was a close connection between competitiveness in the global economy, education, and income. The global labor market, not a limited national labor market, determines the salaries of U.S. workers. All laborers must now compete in a global economy, according to Reich: "Some Americans, whose contributions to the global economy are more highly valued in world markets, will succeed, while others, whose contributions are deemed far less valuable, fail .... Some Americans may command much higher rewards; others, far lower."[35]

Therefore, according to Reich's analysis, raising income levels and overcoming the insecurities of the anxious class requires training people for jobs that are highly rewarded in the global economy. This means changing the education of the entire American workforce. In a global market, "routine production services" are no longer as economically rewarding to American workers as they were in past labor markets. Americans who work in routine production services, which include traditional blue-collar manufacturing, new technology production lines, and data clerks, now compete for wages with workers in Asia, Mexico, Central and South America, and other areas. Consequently, American routine-production workers will either lose their jobs or receive lower wages as multinational corporations search the globe for cheap labor supplies.

What Reich described as "in-person services" are dead-end jobs with low pay and no future. In-person services include the jobs of fast-food employees, janitors, cashiers, hospital attendants and orderlies, and others who provide a direct service. As Reich noted, these jobs require little more than a grade school education and some vocational training. Many workers who are displaced from routine-production jobs find themselves sliding down the wage scale to in-person services.

The top income on Reich's symbolic job list goes to "symbolic-analytical service," which requires a high level of education in the manipulation of symbols—data, visual, oral, and written—and includes the work of research scientists; engineers; public relations experts; investment bankers; real estate developers; accountants; and a whole list of consultants, specialists, managers, and media experts. These are the jobs, according Reich, that command the largest salaries in the global marketplace.

Therefore, within Reich's framework, the ideal economic plan increases incomes for American workers and makes them competitive for global jobs by improving education and training so that workers can compete as symbolic analysts. In addition, Reich contended, this strategy will prevent the increasing inequalities in wealth and income in the United States. In a chapter entitled, "Why the Rich Are Getting Richer and the Poor, Poorer," Reich asserted that "the fortunes of routine producers are declining. In-person servers are also becoming poorer, although their fates are less clear-cut. But symbolic analysts—who solve, identify, and broker new problems—are, by and large, succeeding in the world economy."[36]

Reich admitted that important obstacles may hinder the ability of education to make American workers more competitive. One problem is the tendency for symbolic analysts to protect the educational advantages of their children by living in protected suburban communities with good schools or by sending their children to private schools. In the global economy, educational advantages become a new form of inheritance passed on from generation to generation. Educational inheritance creates a cycle of well-educated families sending their children to good schools to become well educated so they can continue to pass on educational benefits to their children.

In this cycle of educational inheritance the symbolic-analyst class displays little concern for the education of other people's children, particularly those of middle- and low-income working families and the poor. Reich contended that global corporations no longer have a commitment to support the infrastructure of any particular nation. As corporations hop around the globe looking for workers and consumers, the allegiance of the highest paid employees—symbolic analysts—is to their own families and social class. Why should symbolic analysts in India worry about the educational conditions of the Indian masses? Symbolic analysts are mainly concerned with finding top-quality schools for their children. In fact, an overeducated workforce could lead to demands from routine production workers for higher wages or to social unrest.[37]

Shirking their own responsibilities, corporations, according to Reich, demand tax breaks while giving lip service to supporting quality public schools. For example, Reich wrote, "The executives of General Motors, ... who have been among the loudest to proclaim the need for better schools, have also been among the most relentless pursuers of local tax abatements." Reich cited the example of Tarrytown, New York, where a tax break for General Motors resulted in the laying off of schoolteachers.[38]

Consequently, Reich said he hoped corporations will return to an era of corporate responsibility by ensuring quality public schools for all, improving social conditions, and supporting the welfare of their workers. In the global economy, Reich maintained, corporations have lost all sense of corporate responsibility. Corporations move into communities demanding tax breaks that ultimately mean cuts in local school budgets. Corporations abandon communities, leaving behind a crumbling school system and infrastructure. Corporations now downsize and restructure while showing little concern for the welfare of employees and their families. Why should symbolic analysts worry about crumbling communities, abandoned workers, and decaying school systems if they can find a protected suburb of like-minded people and good schools for their children?[39]

The economic program of the New Democrats includes improving corporate responsibility and educational opportunities. In *Between Hope and History* Clinton praised the efforts of the Xerox Corporation for its support of the Urban Family Institute in Washington, DC, which tries to improve the educational futures for at-risk children by providing counseling and emotional support.[40] Clinton proudly recalled the words of Gerald Greenwald, CEO of United Airlines, at a conference on corporate citizenship the administration organized: "Every CEO in America says employees are our most important asset. Well, if that's true, why do we invest more in the overhaul of our machinery than we do in the training … of our employees?"[41]

Hillary Clinton was encouraged by the words of Harvard Business School Professor Michael Porter: "Companies will understand the need to rebuild the corporation and create a sense of community again. The ones that do that will be winners in the next stage of competition."[42] She cited examples of corporate responsibility involving a Cleveland supermarket chain that renovated stores in depressed neighborhoods; an Illinois automotive manufacturer who set aside acres of play space for employee families and provided family-friendly benefits, such as college scholarships, a daycare center, and subsidized tutoring; and a bus company that hired and trained workers who were previously considered unemployable.[43]

The 1996 Democratic national platform emphatically supported the idea of corporations assuming responsibility for the infrastructure of their communities and the welfare of their workers. Under the heading "Corporate Citizenship," the platform stated:

> Employers have a responsibility to do their part as well …. The Democratic Party insists that corporate leaders invest in the long-term, by providing workers with living wages and benefits, education and training, a safe, healthy place to work, and opportunities for greater involvement in

company decision making and ownership. Employers must make sure workers share in the benefits of the good years.[44]

Policies for increasing educational opportunities and gaining corporate commitment are an extension of Clinton's politically successful education policies in Arkansas and his work on Goals 2000. Referring to Bush's education summit and Goals 2000, Clinton gave this reminder to readers of his 1996 campaign book: "In 1989, I and the rest of the nation's governors … were convinced that the more you expect of students, the more they expect of themselves and more they achieve."[45] World-class standards and tests, according to this argument, will increase student achievement and help American workers compete in the global labor market.

Signed by Clinton in 1994, the Goals 2000: Educate America Act and the School-to-Work Act embodied the educational hopes of New Democrats. At the signing of the School-to-Work Act Reich declared, "There should not be a barrier between education and work. We're talking about a new economy in which lifelong learning is a necessity for every single member of the American workforce."[46]

In supporting the Goals 2000: Educate America Act, New Democrats emphasize the unproven assumption that increasing educational standards will improve the schooling of American workers and, consequently, increase wages and decrease economic inequalities. Marshall Smith, speaking at a Brookings Institute conference on national standards 2 months after the signing of the legislation, opened his speech with these remarks:

> The need for American students to learn more demanding content and skills became increasingly clear in the 1980s. The United States faces great challenges: internally, by the need to maintain a strong democracy in a complex and diverse society; externally, by a competitive economic environment that will be dominated by high-skills jobs.[47]

Marshall repeated the unproven maxim of the standards movement that children will learn more if they are challenged by high standards. Concerning Clinton's Goals 2000 legislation, Marshall contended that high academic standards will result in high academic achievement for all students because "it builds on our understanding that all children can learn to higher levels than we have previously thought."[48]

An important assumption of New Democratic strategy is that all students will have equal access to the teachers, books, educational materials, and laboratories required to meet national or state academic standards. The children of symbolic analysts in privileged public or private schools certainly have the opportunity to achieve these standards. Yet what about students attending schools in impoverished rural and urban areas where there is a shortage of textbooks, learning materials, science laboratories, and quality teachers?

Faced with these questions, the New Democrats backtracked to liberal programs of the 1960s and the war on poverty. The 1994 reauthorization of the 1965 Elementary and Secondary Education Act (ESEA), which targeted the problems of "disadvantaged" (a 1960s euphemism for poverty-level) students, was given the hopeful title of the Improving America's Schools Act. According to New Democrats, it was this type of program, with its benefits primarily going to the poor, that drove low- and middle-income voters from the Democratic party. Although focused on helping the same poor population, New Democrats tried to change the legislation's public image by this assertion: "The difference in this reauthorization is that the focus is enhanced opportunities for these students to learn to the same challenging standards as other, more advantaged students."[49]

The Goals 2000: Educate America Act contained a provision to bridge the obvious gap between national and state standards and the "savage inequalities" in the American school system. The Goals 2000 legislation introduced opportunity-to-learn (OTL) standards as "the criteria for … assessing … [the ability] of the education system … to provide all students with an opportunity to learn the material in voluntary national content standards or state content standards."[50] Besides providing for a new area of growth for bureaucrats and educational experts as they tried to achieve "scientific" measurements of school inequalities, the OTL standards held out the hope of finally addressing the issue of inequalities in educational opportunity.

In the past, neoconservatives and New Democrats skillfully avoided the politically charged issue of equal funding of school systems. Currently, state court systems are considering legal suits against inequitable school funding. Upper- and middle-class suburbanites are unwilling to give up their educational advantages, and they are resistant to being taxed to upgrade poorer school districts. As Reich asserted, symbolic analysts are mainly interested in protecting the educational advantages of their children.[51]

The OTL standards were to remedy the inequality problems posed by national and state tests. According to Andrew Porter of the Wisconsin Center for Education Research, one of the federal government's experts hired to make scientific sense of the standard, "The initial motivation for OTL standards stems from an equity concern that high-stakes assessments of student achievement are fair only if students have had an adequate opportunity to learn the content assessed in those high-stakes tests."[52]

As one might have predicted, OTL standards did not fare well in the 1994 Congress in which Republicans, rallying around the Contract With America, vowed to end federal involvement in education and eliminate the Department of Education. This left New Democrat Bill Clinton with only liberal programs, such as ESEA and Head Start, to remedy the most obvious flaw in Goals 2000.

Clinton, therefore, avoided commenting during the 1996 campaign about inequalities in educational opportunity and the educational needs of America's poorest children. Echoing the first goal of Goals 2000, "All children in America will start school ready to learn," Clinton offered the voters expanded funding of Head Start, a liberal and popular program of the 1960s that prepares children from poor families to enter school. Hillary Clinton could offer examples of successful educational projects only for low-income school districts, such as Reading Recovery, the Efficacy Institute, James Comer's family schools, and Education Excellence for Children (EEXCEL). These limited programs with limited funding are hardly answers to the savage inequalities in U.S. schools.

Consequently, the 1996 Democratic campaign focused on making American workers more competitive by expanding college opportunities. "Higher education," the 1996 Democratic national platform proclaimed, "is the key to a successful future in the 21st Century. The typical worker with a college education earns 73% more than one without."[53] This approach offered benefits to middle- and lower income families and avoided the difficult issues of poverty and inequality. Workers' skills were to be upgraded, and Reich's dreams fulfilled, by a combination of tuition tax credits for the first 2 college years, tax deductions for all education after high school, a new GI bill granting $2,600 in tuition grants to unemployed workers, and the continuation of previous Clinton-backed educational legislation providing increased student loans and Pell grants and an opportunity for students to work their way through college by doing community work in Americorps.[54]

ARE THE NEW DEMOCRATS WRONG?
INEQUALITY, EDUCATIONAL INFLATION,
AND SKILLS-MISMATCH THEORY

As suggested earlier, if all students do not have the same opportunity to achieve the knowledge required by national or state standards and achievement tests, then greater economic inequalities might result. New Democrats sincerely believe that expanded educational opportunities will reduce economic inequalities. However, without equal educational opportunity the achievement of national and state standards and the continued use of high-stakes tests can only result in education actually causing greater economic inequalities. Without adequate books, teachers, and educational materials, students in impoverished urban and rural schools systems will not be prepared for high-stakes tests or to reap government benefits for attending college.

Within the current scenario, symbolic analysts will ensure through privileged public or private schools that their children are prepared to pass the high-stakes tests. The anxious class of low- and middle-income families will struggle with public schools of uneven quality to prepare their children for the increasingly important game of getting educational credentials. Impoverished school systems serving poor children might prepare a few students to pass the high-stakes tests, but without greater support Goals 2000 might reduce the possibility of such students graduating from high school.

Of course, there is the problem of educational inflation. The New Democratic assumption is that wages will increase with increased years of education. On the surface this is true, but it is true only if educated workers are scarce. A high school diploma is of greater economic value in a labor market that has only a few high school graduates. However, as the number of high school graduates increases, the economic value of high school diplomas declines. What happens as the number of college graduates increases? In 1994, the Economic Policy Institute announced that for the first time in history the value of a college diploma was declining. In 1993, the median hourly wage for male college graduates declined to $17.62 from an inflation-adjusted high of $18.16 in 1989.[55]

Also, declining wages may be affected by the deskilling of occupations. Many jobs now require less education. Economist David Gordan contends that the spread of computerized machine tools in manufacturing has had no impact on machine shop skill levels. Regarding office occupations, Gordan wrote, "Skill demands appear to have declined substantially—for typists, office equipment, and telephone operators, among others."[56] The increasing inequality in wages between poorly educated and highly educated workers, Gordon argues, is primarily a result of corporate union busting and downsizing.[57] Concerning the assumption that low wages are a result of workers not having the right skills (or skills mismatch), economists Frank Levy and Richard Murnan maintained, "As a positive proposition, evidence of an accelerating skills mismatch is weak." In other words, there is no skill mismatch or lack of skills by American workers if jobs are being deskilled by computerization. Commenting on

Levy and Murnan, Gordon wondered, "Have we found a modern version of the story about the emperor with no clothes?"[58]

New Democrats might respond that the preceding concerns are not meaningful in a global marketplace. Levels of educational attainment should be considered, according to New Democrats, in the context of the world's labor pool. In the New Democratic paradigm, all Americans ideally would receive enough education to become symbolic analysts. There might be a limit, according to this reasoning, on the number of symbolic analysts in the U.S. labor pool, but there might not be a limit in a global labor market. In this scenario, all American workers could earn top wages as symbolic analysts while the rest of world's workers struggle on low wages as routine production workers and in-person servers.

The New Democrats make no promises, except for a modest increase in the minimum wage, to increase wage and job opportunities for routine production workers and in-person servers. Their only promise is to provide educational opportunities so that workers might enter the privileged world of symbolic analysts. Otherwise, the wages and jobs of U.S. workers will vary with the conditions of a global economy. Will this mean that in the 21st century U.S. routine production workers and in-person servers will receive the same wages as comparable workers in Asia, Africa, and Central America? Will the future wages in these occupations be the same worldwide because of declining wages for U.S. workers and increasing wages for workers in poorer countries? Is this the New Democratic vision?

It seems unlikely that existing inequalities in education and the desire of high-income families to protect their educational privileges will give way to conditions in which all Americans can become symbolic analysts. Furthermore, there will probably continue to be a demand in the United States for routine production workers and in-person servers. Of course, like oil-rich Kuwait, the United States could hire foreign workers for these low-paying jobs and reserve the high-paying jobs for Americans.

There are major flaws in the New Democratic dream of decreasing economic inequalities and elevating all Americans to high-income workers in a global labor market. Clinton's strategy of opening college doors for more students will probably increase social mobility for some children of middle- and low-income families. These upwardly mobile college graduates will join the privileged class of symbolic analysts. In contrast, U.S. routine production workers and in-person servers will experience declining wages as they compete with workers in other countries. If educational inequalities are not eliminated, national and state standards and high-stakes tests will doom children of the poor to a world of the underclass.

THE POLITICS OF EDUCATIONAL PSYCHOLOGY

Psychological theories find a political home on the strength of their ideological appeal. This is exemplified by the way the right favors the intelligence theories of *The Bell Curve* by Charles Murray and Richard Herrnstein, whereas the New Democrats approve the intelligence theories of Howard Gardner's *Frames of Mind*. Hillary Clinton recognized the political implications of Herrnstein and Murray's hypotheses. Referring to *The Bell Curve*, she wrote: "This view is politically convenient: If nothing can alter intellectual potential, nothing need be offered to those who begin life with fewer resources or in less favorable environments."[59] As the reader might remember from my discussion of *The Bell Curve* in chapter 2, Hillary Clinton's comments reflect the desire of Herrnstein and Murray to focus educational resources on those with the highest scores for general intelligence.

It is ironic that Herrnstein and Murray's theories could provide a justification for the unintended consequences of New Democratic educational policies. Herrnstein and Murray might counter that symbolic analysts have the highest levels of general intelligence and therefore deserve their high incomes. Also, because they believe one inherits intelligence, these theorists would consider it important for symbolic analysts to protect the educational advantages of their children. Providing increased opportunities to attend college allows children with high IQs, who are born into low- and middle-income or poor families, to cross the line to the world of symbolic analysts. But Herrnstein and Murray argued that it is a waste of public money to provide equal educational opportunities. A high-IQ child from a poor family will make it despite the system. They might contend that the public, however, will not be wasting money by spending it on the education of symbolic analysts' children. From their perspective, the privileged education given to these children will enrich the entire planet. It is ironic that Herrnstein and Murray advanced a theory of intelligence that might justify the unintended effects of the education policies of New Democrats.

Hillary Clinton favors the more upbeat theories of Howard Gardner. The difference between Gardner and Herrnstein and Murray is that Herrnstein and Murray believe in the existence of a measurable general intelligence factor, whereas Gardner discards the idea of general intelligence, preferring the concept of multiple intelligences, such as visual, musical, or mathematical.

In Hillary Clinton's 1996 campaign book *It Takes A Village* she reviewed Gardner's theories and made a plea for ending the practice of schools using IQ tests to label and separate children. In her discussion of Gardner, she concluded that "we would do well to learn to ask how rather than whether someone is smart. That question would shift the emphasis to helping individuals realize their potential, rather than whether they have potential in the first place."[60] Referring to Gardner's theories, Hillary Clinton said she worried about the lack of educational attention given to children labeled as "slow" or "unmotivated." "Tragically," she observed, "the children are thus deprived of the opportunity to master the basic skills they need to realize their particular gifts. This is a loss not only to them but to the entire village, which could benefit from all our talents."[61]

Regarding another set of research findings, both neoconservatives and New Democrats agree on the political implications of effective-schools theory. The attraction of this theory is its claim that high expectations result in greater academic achievement. Translated into the Goals 2000 movement, the theory justifies high national or state academic standards to improve educational achievement. The early source of effective-schools theory was the 1970s study conducted by Robert Rosenthal and Lenore Jackson, "Pygmalion in the Classroom: Teacher Expectation and Pupils' Intellectual Development." Rosenthal and Jackson found that children who were randomly and falsely labeled as having high IQs lived up to this increased expectation by doing better in school. In addition, Michael Rutter in *Fifteen Thousand Hours* reported finding that several factors characterized successful inner-city London schools, including high academic expectations by school officials and teachers.[62]

Diane Ravitch and Chester Finn, Jr., caught the fever of the effective-schools movement when they organized the Educational Excellence Network in 1981 around the following ideas: "Dramatically higher expectations are necessary .... We need tests and assessments that carry stakes and consequences," and "American education should be driven ... by unswerving adherence to standards."[63] Referring to "the plague of low expectations," Hillary Clinton attributed the effective-schools movement to the work of educational leaders such as Theodore Sizer and Ernest Boyer. First on her list of the characteristics of an effective school are "clear expectations that all children can and should learn."[64]

There are problems with using effective-schools research to justify national or state standards. The research focuses on the attitudes of teachers and principals. If teachers have a high expectation for students to learn, then they convey that expectation through innumerable personal ways, such as praise, attention to learning rather than behavior problems, types of questions asked of the students, and an overall belief in the students' abilities.

In contrast, high national or state academic standards do not heighten a teacher's or principal's expectations that a student will learn. Even with high government academic standards, it is still possible for teachers or principals to have low expectations that their students will achieve those standards. Believing that their students are incapable of achieving high academic standards, teachers might completely give up, close the class-room door, and read novels while students entertain themselves. The temptation to give up is certainly always present in overcrowded urban and rural classrooms that lack adequate educational materials.

The confusion between teacher expectations and national standards was evident in Secretary of Education Riley's 1996 State of American Education Address. In a section of the speech entitled "The Challenge to Achieve High Standards," he stated, "We will never help our young people—especially those living in poverty—to measure up if we lower their expectations, water down their curriculum, and write them off by categorizing and stigmatizing them."[65] In the framework of effective-schools research, this sentence was correct only if the *we* in it refers to a student's immediate teachers and school officials. It was not correct in the context of effective schools research if the *we* includes the advo-cates and writers of national standards. There was no research proof that government standards improve academic achievement. The confu-sion between a teacher's expectation that a student can learn and government academic standards can be found throughout discussions of academic standards. There was no necessary relation between a govern-ment's academic expectations and a teacher's belief in a student's ability to achieve those expectations.

Therefore, similar to the use made of Herrnstein, Murray, and Gardner's theories, effective-schools research is used to justify a particular political agenda. Effective-schools research has justified educational poli-cies that embrace the contention that the problem is not money but a lack of high expectations. To parody Marie Antoinette, as poor schools beg for bread, neoconservatives and New Democrats respond, "Give them standards!"

REINVENTING THE GOVERNMENT AND
THE SCHOOL

According to political writer Jacob Weisberg, "The most influential New Democratic idea—and perhaps the only widely read New Democratic book—is *Reinventing Government*."[66] Without adopting an antigovernment stance, David Osborne and Ted Gaebler's *Reinventing Government: How the Entrepreneurial Spirit Is Transforming the Public Sector* gives New Democrats a plan for erasing the Democratic image of being boosters of big government.[67] The essence of the anti-big government solutions offered in *Reinventing Government* is captured in the the following 1996 Democratic national platform declaration: "today's Democratic Party believes in a government that works better and costs less .... We are committed to reinventing government .... The American people do not want big government solutions .... They want a government that ... enhances their quality of life."[68]

Similar to the many tracts by neoconservatives, *Reinventing Government* is a product of the New Democratic think tank, The Progressive Policy Institute. The lead author, David Osborne, is a senior fellow at the institute and served as senior advisor to Gore's National Performance Review, which attempted to reform the federal government. After the publication of *Reinventing Government*, Osborne founded the Reinventing Government Network and the Alliance for Redesigning Government. Osborne's coauthor, Ted Gaebler, is a former city manager.[69]

The basic thesis of *Reinventing Government* is that "the kind of government that developed during the industrial era, with their sluggish, centralized bureaucracies, their preoccupations with rules and regulations, and their hierarchical chains of command, no longer work very well."[70] If the authors had substituted *schools* for *government*, their thesis would have sounded exactly like the warning about obsolescent schools in the 1983 educational report *A Nation at Risk*. On the basis of their discussion of this thesis, Osborne and Gaebler offered suggestions for reinventing government and public schools. Their ideas can be boiled down to seven basic principles:

1. Competition should be created between service providers. For education, this means creating competition between public schools through a choice plan.

2. Citizens should be empowered by transferring control from government bureaucracies to the community. For schools, this means creating for each public school site-based management teams or governance boards consisting of parents, teachers, community members, and school administrators.

3. Outputs rather than inputs should be used to measure government performance. For education, this means rewarding students, teachers, and schools with merit pay for successful grades or student achievement.

4. Missions, not rules and regulations, should guide government agencies. For education, this means being guided by the mission of attaining Goals 2000.

5. Government agencies should consider citizens as customers. For schools, this means choice. Although too recent for Osborne and Gaebler's research, these writers would probably include charter schools in this category.

6. Government should anticipate and prepare for future problems. Although there is no direct discussion of education in this category of government reform, I could imagine educational planners thinking about any potential issues in the education of first graders that might affect these students in high school.

7. Government should be decentralized by replacing hierarchical control with teamwork. For school systems, this means the shifting of decision-making power from a school district's central bureaucracy to a site-based management team at the school level.

In the "Reinventing Public Education" section of their final chapter Osborne and Gaebler stressed the importance of school choice, decentralizing authority, and creating "a system of accountability that focuses on results, rather than compliance on rules and regulations."[71] In this context, state governments and local school boards would set minimum educational standards, enforce social equity, and arrange financing of schools. Anticipating the emergence of charter schools, Osborne and Gaebler underscored this principle: "But the school districts would not operate public schools. Public schools would be run—on something like a contract or voucher basis—by many different organizations: teachers, colleges, even community organizations."[72] Furthermore, they argued, public schools should be encouraged to earn extra tax money by attracting more students in the competitive market created by school choice.

In the spirit of reinvention, the 1996 Democratic national platform called for an expansion of public school choice and the promotion of public charter schools.[73] In harmony with reinventing schools and government, the platform promised to reduce federal regulations and to "give local schools, teachers, and principals the flexibility they need to meet [Goals 2000] standards."[74] Also, Hillary Clinton supported public school choice and public charter schools.[75]

In contrast to the Republican party, the Democratic party stresses that reinvention of school by choice and charters should be limited to public schools. In part, this shows the New Democratic commitment to retaining public control of tax monies. The New Democrats are unwilling to turn public school money over to privately controlled institutions. Their stance also highlights the power of the two teachers' unions. Since the 1970s, the two teachers' unions, with their rich coffers and large memberships, have remained loyal to the Democratic party. These two unions vehemently oppose any choice plan that includes private schools. Currently, the existence of the two unions depends on the continuation of the present public school system. For the same reason, the two teachers' unions oppose privately controlled charter schools, particularly for-profit schools.

Exhibiting the idealism and self-interest of New Democrats and the teachers' unions, the 1996 Democratic national platform urged that tax dollars "should not be taken from public schools and give[n] ... to private schools" and that public charter schools should be "held to the highest standards of accountability and access."[76]

During the first televised Presidential debate on October 6, 1996, Clinton slightly modified his stand on limiting choice to public schools by suggesting that states and local communities could create private school choice plans. However, he felt that this would take money away from public schools. With the ambiguous rhetoric that characterizes political campaigns, Clinton made this statement during the debate:

> I support school choice .... But if you're going to have a private voucher plan, that ought to be determined by states and localities where they're raising and spending most of the money. I simply think it's wrong to take money away from programs that are helping build basic skills for kids—90% of them are in the public schools—to take money away from programs that are helping fund the school lunch program, that are helping to fund the other programs, that are helping schools to improve their standards.[77]

In campaign speeches, Clinton clearly linked charter schools to teacher power and public accountability. After announcing a $1.3 million federal grant for California charter schools, Clinton explained his conception of charter schools at a rally in Rancho Cucamonga on September 12: "[A charter school is] where a group of teachers get together and say 'here's who we're going to serve; here's what we're going to produce; give us a charter and if we don't produce it, take it away from us; hold us accountable'."[78]

MULTICULTURALISM AND AFFIRMATIVE ACTION

New Democrats are in a dilemma regarding multiculturalism. On the one hand, the politics of cultural identity, according to New Democrats, caused many Whites to abandon the Democratic party. On the other hand, many Democrats, including African Americans, Native Americans, Puerto Ricans, Mexican Americans, and gays and lesbians, remain concerned with protecting cultural identities and ensuring civil rights.

Silence is the easiest political solution to this dilemma. Consequently, Clinton has talked about a shared community resulting from common social concerns. There is no suggestion that this community will share the same cultural identity. Hillary Clinton treats multiculturalism as an issue of tolerance. Of course, *tolerance* sounds good, but it is a nebulous word with many shades of meaning. Hillary Clinton concluded, "Yet no matter how hard schools work to teach tolerance and empathy, conflicts will arise, especially when children bring with them different cultural assumptions and expectations."[79] Hillary Clinton recalls her church's youth minister taking her youth group from their suburban community to the inner city of Chicago to share worship and service projects with African American and Latino teenagers. These excursions, Hillary Clinton claims, made her tolerant of other races and cultures.[80]

New Democrats, therefore, tend to reduce the issue of multiculturalism to an education for tolerance. Hillary Clinton applauds programs designed to reduce intolerance and mediate peer disputes. She highlights the work of the Anti-Defamation League and the annual Boston event called Team Harmony in which students, teachers, sports leaders, and businesspeople speak out against prejudice and bigotry. Hillary Clinton considers student responses to Team Harmony as model outcomes for tolerance programs. "Since [Team Harmony]," Hillary Clinton quoted one student as saying, "I want to do all that I can to stop racism .... I don't care that some of my friends are Black, White, Chinese, Vietnamese, or Portuguese."[81]

New Democrats claim that tolerance and racial equality provide an answer to the thorny problem of affirmative action. According to New Democrats, the party lost many White voters because it was identified with affirmative action policies that, in the minds of Whites, gave unfair advantages in hiring and college admissions to members of minority cultures. To win White voters back to the party, New Democrats adopted the position that affirmative action should mean the exercise of racial equality, or "color blindness," as opposed to preferential treatment.

One of Clinton's informal advisors, sociologist William Julius Wilson, affirms the beliefs of New Democrats that affirmative action has been racially divisive and that it has not helped impoverished African Americans.[82] Wilson believes that the problem for many African Americans is not racism but social class. While middle- and low-income African Americans reap the benefits of affirmative action, the underclass, lacking job-related skills, quality schools, and job opportunities, remains stuck in urban ghettos. For Wilson, government policies should focus on helping the underclass of all races, including Whites.[83]

Reflecting Wilson's concern about the divisiveness of affirmative action, Clinton complained, "Affirmative action was intended to give everybody a fair chance, but it hasn't always worked smoothly and fairly."[84] Clinton proposed ending quotas and benefits for those who aren't qualified. He insisted that affirmative action should be based on the idea of giving everyone a chance, "not a guarantee."[85]

GORE AND THE 2000 PRESIDENTIAL CAMPAIGN

During the 2000 Presidential campaign, Gore reiterated the New Democratic vision of public schools preparing workers for the global economy. His published educational agenda linked his positions to those of the Clinton administration. "[Gore]," the 2000 educational agenda stated, "will build on and extend the aggressive efforts since 1993 to improve our schools through higher standards, extra help to students who need it the most, and equal access to higher education."[86] Also, reflecting the human capital arguments of the New Democrats, the 2000 national Democratic platform titled its section on education "Investing in Americans."[87] The stamp of the New Democratic ideology on the purposes of educaton opened this section of the platform: "Democrats know that today, more than ever before, we need the right kinds of investments—in education, lifelong learning, skill development, and research and development—to take advantage of the vast opportunities of the Information Age."[88]

The major changes in Al Gore's 2000 educational agenda, as compared to Clinton's 1992 campaign, were calls for a more expanded role for public schooling and a more detailed approach to changing public schools. The Gore agenda called for the expansion of preschool programs, the creation of second-chance schools for students with serious problems, increased afterschool care, expanded summer school for failing students, and the reformation of failing schools. The last item, the reformation of failing public schools, was strikingly different from Bush's plan to give parents in failing schools vouchers to attend private schools. The Gore agenda also suggested that public schools could be improved with the training of better teachers, creating smaller classrooms and schools, and the empowering of principals to hire their own staff and manage their schools' budgets.

TABLE 4.1
Educational Ideologies

Topic	Religious Right	Neoconservatives	New Democrats
Central concern	Protect the religious beliefs of evangelical Christians.	Implement Austrian free market economics while maintaining the moral and social authority of government.	Protect U.S. workers in a global economy and reduce inequalities in wealth.
Standards and testing	Reject national standards and prefer schools to be based on the Word and intentions of God.	G.W. Bush Republicans favor using the power of the federal government to require states to have a system of assessment.	Favor state standards and testing to ensure that workers will be competitive in a world economy.
Choice	Favor a system that allows parental choice of private religious schools.	Support free competition among public, private, religious, and for-profit schools.	Choice limited to public schools as part of the "reinvention of government."
Charter schools	Favor a charter system that allows for the creation of religious schools.	Favor a charter system that does not recognize collective bargaining agreements of teacher unions and that allows for the chartering of public, religious, and for-profit schools.	Favor charter schools developed within the public school system that give full recognition to collective bargaining agreements.
Multiculturalism	Favor unity through a core set of values based on Christian traditions.	Favor unity around a common core of Anglo-Saxon and/or European values.	Focus on teaching tolerance toward different cultural groups.

CONCLUSION

At the risk of oversimplification, I conclude this chapter with Table 4.1, which shows the differing educational interests of the religious right, neoconservatives, and New Democrats. In examining this table the reader should remember that these differing educational concerns reflect conflicting political strategies and ideologies. For instance, the New Democrats developed a political strategy to win back voters from the Republican party. In addition, New Democrats believe that Goals 2000 has an important role to play in reducing inequality of wealth in the United States by giving workers skills that are competitive in a global economy. To achieve this goal, the New Democrats call for the reinvention of the public schools through public school choice and charter schools.

The same combination of strategy and beliefs is evident with the religious right and neoconservatives. As discussed in chapter 1, the Christian Coalition's leader, Ralph Reed, openly acknowledges that the coalition's alliance with the Republican party is purely a marriage of convenience to protect the religious beliefs of its members by promoting a system of public–private choice and charter schools. Until the Contract With America and the Christian Coalition's control of the 1996 Republican platform, neoconservatives felt comfortable working within the Republican party. Neoconservatives primarily interested in free market economics could support the 1996 Republican ticket because of the presence of Jack Kemp, but neoconservatives wanting to support Goals 2000 had to turn to the Democratic party, even though they objected to the Democratic party's limitation of choice and charters to public schools. In contrast, neoconservatives favor parents and students choosing from a free market of private, religious, for-profit, and public schools.

NOTES

1. Richard Riley, "State of American Education Address," 28 February 1996 (Washington, DC: Office of the Secretary of Education, 1996), 11.

2. Ibid.

3. "2000 Democratic National Platform," *New York Times on the Web*, 17 August 2000, p. 7. Available: www.nytimes.com

4. David Rosenbaum, "Bush and Gore Stake Claims to Federal Role in Education," *New York Times on the Web*, 30 August 2000. Available: www.nytimes.com

5. See John Hale, "The Making of the New Democrats," Democratic Leadership Council home page, http://www.dlcppi.com.

6. John Hale, "The People Behind the Ideas at the Progressive Policy Institute," Democratic Leadership Council home page, http://www.dlcppi.com.

7. Ted Kolderie, "Beyond Choice to New Public Schools: Withdrawing the Exclusive Franchise in Public Education," *Policy Report*, November 1990, No. 8, 3. Available: http://www.dlcppi.com.

8. Ibid., 13.

9. Alison Mitchell, "They See the Future and It Works for Them," *New York Times*, 11 October 1996, A26.

10. Ibid.

11. "The Gore Agenda: Revolutionizing American Education in the 21st Century." Available: http://www.gore2000.org.

12. "2000 Democratic National ... ," 16.

13. Ibid., 15–16.

14. Meredith L. Oakley, *On the Make: The Rise of Bill Clinton* (Washington, DC: Regnery, 1994), 275.

15. Ibid., 277.

16. Ibid., 287.

17. Ibid., 291.

18. Ibid., 313, 328, 406.

19. Jacob Weisberg, *In Defense of Government: The Fall and Rise of Public Trust* (New York: Scribner's, 1996), 132.

20. Bill Clinton & Al Gore, *Putting People First: How We Can All Change America* (New York: Times Books, 1992), 3.

21. The Report of the Platform Committee to the 1996 Democratic National Convention, The 1996 Democratic National Platform (1996), p. 1.

22. Katherine Seelye, "Dole Uses Clinton Health Plan to Portray Him as a Liberal," *New York Times*, 24 September 1996, A20.

23. Hillary Rodham Clinton, *It Takes a Village and Other Lessons Children Teach Us* (New York: Simon & Schuster, 1996), 312.

24. Ibid., 308.

25. Ibid., 307.

26. Bill Clinton, *Between Hope and History: Meeting America's Challenges for the 21st Century* (New York: Times Books, 1996), 6–7.

27. Ibid., 7.

28. Clinton & Gore, *Putting People First*, 86.

29. Ibid., 85.

30. "Clinton's Speech Accepting the Democratic Nomination for President," *New York Times*, 30 August 1996, A20.

31. Ibid.

32. Ibid.

33. Bill Clinton, *Between Hope and History*, 29.

34. Hillary Clinton, *It Takes a Village*, 294.

35. Robert Reich, *The Work of Nations: Preparing Ourselves for 21st-Century Capitalism* (New York: Knopf, 1991), 173.

36. Ibid., 208.
37. Ibid., 268–300.
38. Ibid., 281.
39. Ibid., 261–300.
40. Bill Clinton, *Between Hope and History*, 60.
41. Ibid., 51.
42. Hillary Clinton, *It Takes a Village*, 301.
43. Ibid., 300.
44. 1996 Democratic National Platform, 12.
45. Bill Clinton, *Between Hope and History*, 42.
46. Lynn Olson, "President Signs a School-to-Work Act," *Education Week*, 11 May 1994, 1, 21.
47. Marshall S. Smith, *Education Reform in America's Public Schools: The Clinton Agenda*, in Diane Ravitch (Ed.), *Debating the Future of American Education: Do We Need National Standards and Assessments?* (Washington, DC: Brookings Institution, 1995), 9.
48. Ibid., 10.
49. Ibid., 23.
50. Smith, *Education Reform*, 40. The legislation is quoted by Andrew Porter, "The Uses and Misuses of Opportunity-to-Learn Standards" in Ravitch (Ed.), *Debating the Future of American Education: Do We Need National Standards and Assessments?* (Washington, DC: Brookings Institution, 1995), 41.
51. As an example of how long the attempt has been made in the courts to achieve equality of spending between school districts, check Richard Lehne's now-dated book, *The Quest for Justice: The Politics of School Finance Reform* (New York: Longman, 1978). Jonathan Kozol's *Savage Inequalities: Children in America's Schools* (New York: Crown, 1991) is still the best denunciation of the lack of opportunity to learn in many U.S. schools.
52. Porter, "The Uses and Misuses," 41.
53. 1996 Democratic National Platform, 8.
54. Descriptions and justifications of these programs can be found in Bill Clinton, *Between Hope and History*, 43–52, and the 1996 Democratic National Platform, 7–9.
55. See Louis Uchitelle, "A Degree's Shrinking Returns," *New York Times*, 5 September 1994, 33–45.
56. David M. Gordon, *Fat and Mean: The Corporate Squeeze of Working Americans and the Myth of Managerial "Downsizing"* (New York: Free Press, 1996), 184.
57. Ibid., 175–187.
58. Quote of Ibid., 187.
59. Hillary Clinton, *It Takes a Village*, 59.
60. Ibid., 242–243.
61. Ibid., 240–241.
62. Michael Rutter, *Fifteen Thousand Hours* (Cambridge, MA: Harvard University Press, 1979); Robert Rosenthal and Lenore Jackson, *Pygmalion in the Classroom: Teacher Expectation and Pupils' Intellectual Development* (New York: Irvington, 1988).
63. "The Educational Excellence Network." Available: http://www.al.com/hudson/, 1.

64. Hillary Clinton, *It Takes a Village*, 248.

65. Riley, "State of American Education Address," 7.

66. Weisberg, *In Defense of Government*, 133.

67. David Osborne & Ted Gaebler, *Reinventing Government: How the Entrepreneurial Spirit Is Transforming the Public Sector* (New York: Penguin, 1993).

68. The 1996 Democratic National Platform, 1, 4.

69. Hale, "The Making of the New Democrats," 3.

70. Osborne & Gabler, *Reinventing Government,* 11–12.

71. Ibid., 315.

72. Ibid., 316.

73. Ibid., 7.

74. The 1996 Democratic National Platform, 6.

75. Hillary Clinton, *It Takes a Village*, 263.

76. The 1996 Democratic National Platform, 7.

77. "A Transcript of the First Televised Debate Between Clinton and Dole," *New York Times*, 7 October 1996, B10.

78. Paul Basken, "Clinton Talking Education in California," United Press International, Compuserve, Executive News Service, 12 September 1996, 1, italics added.

79. Hillary Clinton, *It Takes a Village*, 190.

80. Ibid., 176–177.

81. Ibid., 193.

82. For a discussion of Wilson's role as an informal advisor to Bill Clinton, see Sean Wilentz's review, "Jobless and Hopeless," *New York Times Book Review*, 29 September 1996, 7.

83. William J. Wilson, *The Declining Significance of Race: Blacks and Changing American Institutions* (Chicago: University of Chicago Press, 1979).

84. Bill Clinton, *Between Hope and History*, 132.

85. Ibid.

86. "The Gore Agenda ... "

87. "2000 Democratic National ... ," 7.

88. Ibid.

Chapter 5

What's Left of the Left?
Ralph Nader and the
Green Party

◆ ◆ ◆

In the first edition of this book this chapter emphasized the disarray existing among the differing factions of the "left" in the United States. However, in the 2000 Presidential election the left rallied around Green Party candidate Ralph Nader. A longtime consumer advocate, Nader was the first U.S. Presidential candidate to focus on the problems associated with a consumerist ideology. Nader's educational concern was with the impact of consumerist ideology on children and teenagers and the resulting undermining of democratic activism.

Nader and many other members of the left now consider consumerism to be the triumphant ideology of the modern world and globalization.[1] It is consumerism, and not capitalism, they argue, that won the Cold War of the 20th century. Consumerism defeated communist ideology in the Soviet Union because, quite simply, the Soviet government's economic planning could not produce consumer goods as well as the West.

Consumerist ideology assumes that the goal of the economic system are constant growth and consumption of products. Constant economic growth and consumption are considered devastating to the environment and the quality of human life. Within this framework the goal of technological development is the production of new goods.

The production of new goods requires the creation of new human needs. The development of advertising techniques in the United States in the early 20th century, and the global spread of these techniques in the 20th and 21st centuries, is the agency for developing these new needs. Economists, such as Simon Patten in the early 20th century, argued that agricultural and industrial development would continually produce surpluses of products. The only way the agricultural and industrial machinery could be maintained, Patten argued, was the creation of new needs. Later, corporations, such as General Motors, introduced the idea of planned obsolescence through advertising new styles and models.

Consequently, advertising not only creates a need for new products but also convinces consumers to abandon products that they own for similar products with different styling. Within the framework of the ideology of consumerism, personal identity and social status are attached to brand names. People proudly wear clothes with identifying brand names or drive cars that identify their personality or social status.

Working and spending are the central values of consumerist ideology. Constant consumption requires longer hours of work: This is the tragic irony of consumerism. Technological advances do not free people from work but instead make new products that require more work to purchase. For instance, technology could be used to produce durable goods and reduce hours at work.

Commodified leisure, as exemplified by movies, television, Disney World, video games, recreational products, and packaged travel, provide both an escape from work and a reason to work harder. People work harder so that they can buy such items as boats, golf clubs, the newest hiking gear, and tickets for travel on a cruise ship. The desire for commodified leisure fills the fantasy world of the worker. In turn, the consumption of leisure provides escape from the often-numbing quality of office and factory work.

What distinguishes capitalism from consumerism? Capitalism assumes that people make rational choices in a free market, whereas consumerism assumes that individual choices in the market are a result of the manipulation of desires. In turn, political choices are the result of the manipulation of desires through the media. Politicians rely on advertising, media experts, and spin doctors to present their political agenda. Political image takes the place of political substance.

RALPH NADER, CONSUMERISM, AND EDUCATION

During the 2000 Presidential campaign, Nader made consumerism the focal point of his educational policy statements. In his acceptance speech as Presidential candidate of the Green party on June 25, 2000, Nader argued that there is a responsibility "to ensure that our children are well cared for. This is an enormous undertaking because our children are now exposed to the most intense marketing onslaught in history."[2] This marketing offensive, Nader argued, involves "precise corporate selling ...

beamed directly to children separating them from their parents, an un-heard of practice formerly, and teaching them how to nag their belea-guered parents as unpaid salesman for companies. There is a bombard-ment of their impressionable minds."[3]

Nader linked the lack of political activism and concern among youth to the commercialization of their minds. He argued that commodified lei-sure occupies more and more of children's time. This results, Nader con-tended, in youth not responding to the growing economic inequalities in the United States and between nations. "To the youth of America," Nader warned in his acceptance speech, "beware of being trivialized by the commercial culture that tempts you daily. I hear you saying often that you're not turned on to politics .... If you do not turn on to politics, poli-tics will turn on you."[4]

Concern about political activism is a key element in the Green party agenda. The Green party's position on government reform is sometimes hard for citizens to understand, because the word *democracy* has fre-quently been used to describe the U.S. government system. The confu-sion is over the differences between representative government and di-rect democracy. The democratic aspect of representative government is the right of citizens to vote for their representatives. The Green party be-lieves that elected representatives limit the ability of citizens to decide important issues. The 1996 Green platform explained it in these words:

> Greens advocate direct democracy as a response to local needs and issues, where all concerned citizens can discuss and decide questions that imme-diately affect their lives, such as land use, parks, schools and community services. We hold as a "key value" GRASSROOTS DEMOCRACY and, as such, would decentralize many state functions to the country level and seek expanded roles for neighborhood boards/associations.[5]

For Nader, commodified leisure was both reducing political activity and interfering with the ability of children to learn. Nader argued, "Obvi-ously, you see how our children are not learning enough history, they're not learning how to write. Their attention span is being shrunken by all this entertainment on TV and videos that are beamed to them."[6] In his nomination speech he contended that, "This does not prepare the next generation to become literate, self-renewing, effective citizens for a delib-erative democracy."[7]

The problem, as Nader defined it, was corporate targeting of children as present and future consumers. He quoted Mike Searles, former presi-dent of Kids-R-Us: "If you own this child at an early age, you can own this child for years to come. Companies are saying, 'Hey, I want to own the kid younger and younger'."[8] To prove his point, he quoted a *Los Angeles Times* interview with Nancy Shalek, president of the Shalek Agency: "Advertising at its best is making people feel that without their product, you're a loser. Kids are very sensitive to that .... You open up emotional vulnerabilities and it's very easy to do with kids because they're the most emotionally vulnerable."[9]

The undermining of parental authority, according to Nader, was the goal of advertisers and their paid child psychologists. The process begins as early as age 2, with companies marketing directly to children. Boys and girls under the age of 12, Nader claimed, were responsible for the spending of $25 billion a year. Nader contended that marketers use three methods to "avoid or neutralize parental authority:"

- First, they urge the child to nag the parents.
- Second, the sellers take conscious advantage of the absence of parents who are commuting and working long hours away from home.
- Third, the marketers know that if they can undermine the authority, dignity, and judgment of parents in the eyes of their children, the little ones will purchase or demand items regardless of their parents' opinions.

In addition to being disturbed by the undermining of democracy by training of present and future consumers, Nader was disturbed by the effects of advertising and media on the present and future health of children. For instance, he argued that there was a direct link between teenage drinking and car crashes, suicide, date rapes, and problems teenagers have had in school and with their parents. Despite these problems, the alcohol industry advertises to audiences, according to the Federal Trade Commission, that include children and places their products in PG and PG-13 films that appeal to children and teenagers. In addition, the alcohol industry advertised on 8 of the 15 television shows that were most popular with adolescents. Advertising led to teenage smoking, for instance, the Marlboro Man, Nader claimed, appealed to teenage desires for independence.[11]

Violence is, Nader contends, presented to children and teenagers through movies, television, and video games. Nader quoted Lt. Col. Grossman, coauthor of *Stop Teaching Our Kids to Kill*, that shooter video games such as Duke Nukem, Time Crisis, and Quake "teach children the motor skills to kill, like military training devices do. And then they turn around and teach them to like it like the military would never do."[12]

Also, according to Nader, children's health has been undermined by a "barrage of ads for Whoppers, Happy Meals, Coke, Pepsi, Snickers bars, M&M's, and other junk foods and fast foods."[13] These marketing efforts contribute to the rise of child and teenage obesity and diabetes. Heath risks associated with severe obesity among children, Nader claimed, doubled since the 1960s. Now, he argued, 25%–30% of children are clinically obese.

Nader criticized schools for developing a consumer culture. He pointed to the widespread use of Chris Whittle's Channel 1 broadcasts in classrooms around the country. Whittle, it should be noted, is also the major stockholder in the for-profit school franchise the Edison Project. The program reaches, according to Nader, 8 million middle, junior high, and high school students in 12,000 schools. The total time spent by students watching Channel 1 in 1 year was equivalent to about 1 class week. A 10-minute news broadcast on Channel 1 contained 2 minutes of commercials. Joel Babbit, former president of Channel 1, stated that "we are forcing kids to watch two minutes of commercials."[14]

Nader's criticism of Channel 1 contains a basic criticism of consumerist ideology. Nader argued, "What Channel One really conveys is materialism: that buying is good and will solve your problems, and that consumption and self-gratification are the goals and ends of life."[15] Nader argued that many of Channel 1 commercials

promote low-grade sensuality to children as young as 11. Chew Winterfresh gum and kiss the Winterfresh babe. Shave with Schick razors and the Schick babe will hug you. There are ads for Blockbuster Video that portray kids playing video games nonstop for five days until they pass out from exhaustion. A Mountain Dew ad glorifies reckless driving. A Twix candy bar ad shows kids avoiding the consequences of doing badly at school by sending their report cards to the Eskimos so their parents won't read them. There are ads for Snickers that encourage kids to eat junk food. And then there are the ads, for products such as Gatorade, that show skinny models that make teenage girls feel badly about the way they look and encourage an unhealthy body image and an obsession with being thin.[16]

What is Nader's answer to the destruction of democracy through the commercialization of the minds of children and teenagers? First, he has argued that Congress should repeal Public Law 96-252, which prohibits the Federal Trade Commission from establishing rules to the protect children from commercial advertising. Second, he has appealed for a coalition of groups, including conservative organizations such as the Eagle Forum and Family Research Council, to work for laws to protect children from advertising and limit the access of marketing groups such as Channel 1 to public schools. Third, he has urged citizens to join the Center for a New American Dream, which is dedicated to overthrowing the ideology of consumerism. He recommended that citizens obtain the Center for a New American Dream's pamphlet, "Tips for Parenting in a Commercial Culture."

The Nader campaign also stressed the issue of child poverty, contending that 20% of children in the U.S. lived in poverty—a figure much higher than that for any other Western country. In addition, there is a direct link, Nader contended, between childhood poverty and school performance and, consequently, expectations for future earnings. Childhood poverty contributes, Nader argued, to the perpetuation of poverty. Nader called for more expanded health and welfare programs for children that would be paid for out of the future budget surplus of the federal government. Attacking Gore's Presidential candidacy, Nader argued that Gore proposed to "spend 88 percent of the projected budget surplus over the next decade on three accounts: Medicare, Social Security and private pension subsidies. Children are clearly not a priority. They are given only lip service and symbolic federal programs—and photo opportunities."[17]

Nader was the first Presidential candidate to directly attack the ideology of consumerism and propose an educational agenda that included the protection of children and teenagers from indoctrination into consumerist values. This protection was to be combined with the teaching of an anticonsumerist ideology that included environmental education. In addition, Nader urged government programs to eliminate childhood poverty. The combination of these efforts, Nader believed, would result in a generation dedicated to hands-on participation in democratic processes.

WHAT'S LEFT OF THE LEFT?

Did Nader's 2000 campaign unite the left? Picking over the bones of the liberal wing of the Democratic party, Michael Tomasky, author and political commentator for *The Village Voice* and *New York* magazine, searched for policies that would restore to the left a cohesive political agenda. In *Left for Dead*, he contended that the liberal left's political efforts are hampered because that by "speaking to people as members of groups—and only as members of groups—we've lost the ability to talk to the whole."[18] Using *left*, *liberal left*, and *progressive* interchangeably, Tomasky described the political dilemmas facing a wheelchair-bound African American lesbian. Which of her four identities—disabled, African American, woman, and lesbian—defines her politics? She has, Tomasky pointed out, other identities as a worker, commuter, purchaser of goods, renter or home-owner, and neighbor. "The left," Tomasky complained, "has been dogged about addressing her identity as female, Black, lesbian, and disabled, far less so about addressing the others."[19]

Tomasky's quest for a means of reunifying the left is in response to the abandonment of the Democratic party by voters who were alienated by the attention given to the poor and disenfranchised groups. What politi-cal policies can unite disparate groups, such as the wheelchair-bound Af-rican American lesbian, the African American male auto worker, the White female small farmer, and the Latina female office worker? Al-though he is aware of the special issues for minority cultures, women, gays and lesbians, and the disabled, Tomasky hopes that broader issues can be found to unite the progressive wing of the Democratic party.

What does Tomasky offer as the salvation of the liberal left? "The first principle," he proposed, "is to fight the new war: to produce a strategy to protect working families in the age of globalization."[20] Like the New Democrats, Tomasky recognizes that the development of a global work-force is depressing U.S. wages. Yet, unlike the New Democrats, Tomasky does not want the global labor market to victimize workers. Tomasky is sickened by corporate leaders earning 45 times more than the wage of av-erage workers. He suggests protecting workers by reducing the work week to 30 hours, giving workers control of their companies, reducing federal programs that provide welfare to corporations, increasing corporate taxes, reducing taxes on annual incomes below $80,000, and increasing taxes on incomes above $80,000. Higher corporate taxes—which declined over the last 40 years, from 38% to 13%—and taxes on high incomes, Tomas-ky maintains, would pay for reduced taxes on low incomes and govern-ment programs that would give U.S. workers adequate medical care, better public schools, and secure retirement programs. Topping the list of Tomasky's proposals for government reform is breaking the influence of money over political campaigns and legislative decisions. Regarding per-sonal freedom, Tomasky supports gay and lesbian rights, freedom of speech, and the legal access to abortion.[21]

Tomasky offers a small agenda for uniting the left around school is-sues. Multiculturalism—despised by the right and ignored by New Demo-crats—continues as an important subject for progressives. Tomasky wants textbooks to include more history and information on minority cultures. "But this history," he insisted, "should be taught not out of pietistic con-cern for the self-esteem of minority children, as the left has posited, but simply because it is information that all American children, all future citizens should have."[22] Tomasky wants the left to assume leadership in raising academic standards and lengthening the school day and school year.

THE RAINBOW COALITION

"Democrats for the Leisure Class"—that is what Jesse Jackson calls the Democratic Leadership Council.[23] As founder and national field director of the Rainbow Coalition, Jackson is an outspoken critic of efforts by the Democratic Leadership Council and the New Democrats to push the Democratic party to the center of the political spectrum. Running for the Democratic Presidential nomination in 1984, he tried to keep the party focused on liberal concerns about the rights of labor, inequalities in wealth, and racial and gender equity.[24] From Jackson's perspective, "the Democratic Leadership Conference [sic]—'the moderate' Democratic organization [that was] formed to offset the influence of the National Rainbow Coalition after the 1984 presidential campaign ... [wanted] to appeal to white males and pull the Democratic Party back to the center."[25]

Losing the struggle over the direction of the Democratic party to the New Democrats, Jackson remained the best-known progressive voice in the Democratic party. Jackson warned that "the only counter to prevent Clinton from caving in to the Republican right and conservatives in his own party, if he is to be countered, is his base—people of color, workers, women and progressives."[26]

As the progressive voice of the Democratic party Jackson is outspoken in his criticism of the Christian Coalition. He charges the Christian Coalition with being an exclusionary organization and observed that "their mean-spiritedness is not limited to Blacks. There are no Jews in the 'Christian Coalition,' by definition."[27] Warning of the dangers of the right, Jackson asserted, "If this were Germany, we would call it fascism. If this were South Africa, we would call it apartheid. In America we call it conservatism. And it provides a cover for a public policy of scapegoating, exclusion, and distrust."[28]

Regarding education, Jackson and the Rainbow Coalition support a continuation of the 1960s' liberal education agenda, including war-on-poverty programs, affirmative action, remedial education, Head Start, day care, and parental involvement in schools. This liberal model assumes that equality of educational opportunity is the key to providing economic opportunity. On the surface, the Rainbow Coalition's educational policies are similar to those of the New Democrats. Below the surface are profound differences.

Affirmative action is one important difference. Hoping to win back White men to the Democratic party, New Democrats support a race- and gender-neutral policy for affirmative action. In contrast, the Rainbow Coalition and their ally, the National Organization for Women (NOW), reject a race- and gender-neutral policy. The leaders of these two organizations want affirmative action to correct racial and gender imbalances by considering existing balances. For instance, if a college does not have any African American faculty members, then the college should actively recruit African Americans. A race- and gender-neutral policy would not try to correct existing racial and gender imbalances; instead it would try to avoid racial and gender discrimination. Throughout this chapter I use the term *positive affirmative action* to indicate policies that consciously attempt to correct existing imbalances.

Affirmative action as a legal policy originated with the passage of the 1964 Civil Rights Act, which prohibited discrimination based on race, color, religion, sex, or national origin. In 1965, President Lyndon Johnson issued an executive order requiring federal agencies to "maintain a positive program of equal opportunities."[29] A "positive program" was interpreted to mean that the race and gender of a job applicant should be considered during the hiring process in order to achieve a fair racial and gender balance in employment.

According to the Rainbow Coalition and NOW, equal educational opportunity is rendered meaningless unless there are positive affirmative-action hiring practices. Equal educational opportunity is also meaningless unless there are positive affirmative-action college admission policies. If there are no positive affirmative-action programs for hiring faculty members, then female and racial minority students are denied positive role models in elementary and secondary schools and colleges.

Both the Rainbow Coalition and NOW contend that there is legal precedent for positive affirmative-action policies in education. In the famous Bakke decision, the U.S. Supreme Court, while ruling against the affirmative-action admissions policy of the medical school of the University of California, found that "race conscious" admissions policies were constitutional. In 1989, the U.S. Supreme Court ruled as constitutional the affirmative-action hiring program of the Aluminum and Chemical Corporation that set aside half its trainee positions for African Americans until racial parity was reached. Other affirmative-action quota programs have also been ruled constitutional.[30]

Therefore, unlike the New Democrats, the Rainbow Coalition considers positive affirmative-action programs essential for ensuring equality of educational opportunity and equality of opportunity in the workplace as well as for providing racial minorities and women with positive role models in educational institutions.

Unlike many on the right, the Rainbow Coalition retains a belief in the possibility of equal educational opportunity overcoming educational problems caused by poverty. The debate sparked by Richard Herrnstein and Charles Murray's book *The Bell Curve* underscores the differing attitudes regarding education and poverty. Hillary Clinton, as discussed in chapter 4, dismissed Herrnstein and Murray's claim of an inheritable general intelligence while accepting Howard Gardner's theory of multiple intelligence. As Hillary Clinton sees it, Herrnstein and Murray's theory provides an excuse for denying educational opportunities to children from low-income families.

Jesse Jackson's condemnation of Herrnstein and Murray is much harsher than that of Hillary Clinton. Under the colorful title "Let Them Eat Grits: Pseudo-Intellect Mixes Race, IQ to Justify America's Ethnic Cleansing," Jackson asserted that "Charles Murray has cleverly packaged and promoted a new book that will be an unread bestseller .... The conservative polemicist will pocket a small fortune huckstering a pseudointellectual justification for the affluent to feel no responsibility for the wretched." Using what Jackson calls pseudoscientific methods, Herrnstein and Murray not only relieved the rich of any guilt about the poor but justified beliefs that "attempts to alleviate their misery are doomed to failure. Affirmative action should be repealed, remedial education abandoned."[31]

In his review of *The Bell Curve* Jackson argued that paying for the Vietnam war reduced funding for the war on poverty and destroyed any possibility of its success. The continued cost of the cold war, or what Jackson called "the most expensive peace time military buildup in the annals of time," further exacerbated the problem of poverty. "Those in barrios and ghettos," Jackson complained, "were left more segregated and wretched than ever. Today 45% of all Black children live at or below poverty in destructive conditions lacking prenatal care, nutrition, immunization, safe homes, decent neighborhoods."[32]

To save children living in poverty, Jackson argues, requires full funding of war-on-poverty programs or, as Jackson stated, "Why not earn and learn our way out of poverty?" In 1993, Jackson initiated the Rainbow National Reclaim Our Youth Crusade to build self-esteem and give direction to young people. In 1994, the organization created a Back-To-School Pledge asking a promise from parents to accompany their children on the first day of school, meet the child's teachers, pick up report cards, and turn off the television for 3 hr a night. Another organizational proj-

ect, the Youth Empowerment Committee, creates opportunities for youth
to investigate and debate issues involving urban poverty, while the
Courts and Justice Committee attempts to keep youth out of jail.[33]

Fulfilling of the liberal agenda of the war on poverty, Jackson believes,
is possible. Adequate prenatal care for women, good nutrition, and medical care for infants combined with quality Head Start and daycare programs will, Jackson argues, give children born into poverty an equal opportunity to learn when they enter school. Remedial education programs
will help children overcome learning problems. The Back-To-School
Pledge will foster parental involvement in education and ensure that the
home supports the work of the school. To complete the Rainbow Coalition's educational agenda, positive affirmative-action policies will ensure
that faculties can provide positive role models for all students, that school
graduates are given an equal opportunity to enter college, and that equal
educational opportunities result in an equal opportunity to get a job.

THE NATIONAL ORGANIZATION FOR WOMEN AND
THE FEMINIST MAJORITY

"There is no civil rights movement to speak for women as there has been
for Negroes and other victims of discrimination. The National Organization for Women must therefore begin to speak."[34] With these historic
words in 1966, NOW joined the civil rights movement and assumed political leadership that would transform public schools.

Like the Rainbow Coalition, NOW is critical of the New Democratic
movement. Describing its membership as "feminists and progressives" at a
1996 demonstration in front of the White House, NOW president Patricia Ireland ridiculed Contract-With-America Republicans and Bill
Clinton for the passage and signing of new welfare legislation. "The so-
called 'pro-family' Congress," Ireland proclaimed, "churned out a law that
will destroy poor families. And now the so-called 'new Democrat' in the
White House signed it."[35] After attacking the Republican Congress and
the New Democrats, Ireland turned her attention to the power of the religious right with these words: "Bill Clinton is only the most recent politician to stagger to the right after an onslaught of immoral attacks by the
highly organized religious and political extremists, ... and we see the radical right's ability to raise money and defeat progressive candidates—often
with the aid and assistance of churches."[36]

At a "Fight the Right" San Francisco rally in 1996, Ireland acknowledged unity with other progressive organizations, including the Rainbow
Coalition, in opposing the religious right, neoconservatives, and the New

Democrats. Of particular concern to NOW was the attempt to end positive affirmative-action policies. "In California, the Congress and everywhere in between," Ireland declared, "we're going to squash the right wing's jaded attempt to roll back decades of progress on affirmative action and other issues. The vehemence of their attacks is an ironic indicator of our success over the years."[37]

Ireland's reference to "our success" is an accurate evaluation of NOW's accomplishments in schools and colleges. Over the years, NOW has been a strong political force for the following goals:

1. Ensuring equal access for women to educational programs such as science, mathematics, vocational, and athletics.
2. Creating nonsexist learning materials.
3. Creating learning materials that increase female's self-esteem.
4. Breaking down the exclusionary walls of all-male schools.
5. Establishing women's studies programs.
6. Reducing the sexist bias in high-stakes tests.
7. Creating affirmative-action college admission programs for women.
8. Creating affirmative-action faculty-hiring programs.
9. Protecting female faculty members from discriminatory practices in the college tenure process.

The 1966 Statement of Purpose, coauthored by Betty Friedan, author of *The Feminine Mystique,* and Dr. Pauli Murray, an African American Episcopal minister, placed NOW's educational efforts in a general struggle to achieve "a fully equal partnership of the sexes ... [and a] full participation [of women] in the mainstream of American society ... exercising all the privileges and responsibilities thereof in truly equal partnership with men."[38] Friedan and Murray contended that women with an average life span of nearly 75 years no longer devote the greatest part of their lives to childrearing. Furthermore, they asserted, muscular strength, because of technological advances, is no longer "a criterion for filling most jobs."[39] Therefore, they argued, "In view of this new industrial revolution created by automation in the mid-twentieth century, women must participate in old and new fields of society in full equality—or become permanent outsiders."[40] The Statement of Purpose provided evidence of sex segregation in the labor market, discriminatory wage differences between men and women, and the small numbers of women as compared to men graduating from college and professional schools. In response to these data, Friedan and Murray called for the effective enforcement of American law and the Constitution to end patterns of sex discrimination, to provide equality of civil and political rights, and "to ensure equality of opportunity in employment and education."[41]

Calling education "the key to effective participation in today's economy," the writers of NOW's original Statement of Purpose demanded that public schools educate every young woman "to her full potential of human ability."[42] Of primary concern to the writers was raising female expectations for achievement in school and for pursuing professional degrees. The document identified the following educational problems confronting women:

1. Discriminatory quotas in college and professional school admissions.
2. Lack of encouragement by parents, counselors, and teachers.
3. Denial of fellowships and loans to women.
4. Traditional procedures in professional training geared to men.
5. Lack of attention to female school dropouts.

NOW's Task Force on Education issued its report in 1967. The report's primary concern was to raise the aspiration levels of females at every level of schooling and limit the influence of traditional sex-oriented self-concepts. Besides changing the sex-role stereotypes found in schools, the task force commended the activities of the NOW Task Force on Media. The NOW Task Force on Education proposed placing articles in professional journals, pressuring school administrators, and contacting parents and the Parent–Teacher Association.[43]

The turning point in NOW's education efforts came in 1972 with the passage of Title IX of the Higher Education Act. The legislation provided for sexual equality in all educational institutions, including preschool classrooms, elementary and secondary schools, vocational and professional schools, and public and private undergraduate and graduate schools. Armed with the legal power of Title IX, NOW began a national campaign for its enforcement. Local NOW chapters sued local school systems. The first important lawsuit by a local chapter of NOW was against the 13 school systems in Essex County, New Jersey. The local NOW chapter accused the school systems of maintaining sex-segregated courses in home economics and industrial arts.[44]

In 1974, NOW defeated efforts by the National Collegiate Athletic Association to omit sports from the coverage of Title IX. Consequently, 1975 federal regulations were created to bar sex discrimination in intercollegiate athletics. By 1976, NOW chapters across the country were using Title IX in lawsuits ranging from female participation in athletics to gender-biased hiring in school administration. Also, in 1975, NOW'S Legal and Defense Fund charged 40 states with violating federal requirements under Title IX.

By 1974, with help from NOW's Committee to Promote Women's Studies, more than 1,000 colleges were offering women's studies courses and degree programs. Also, NOW began pressuring Congress for legislation allowing admission of women to military service academies. Under political pressure from NOW and other women's organizations, Congress passed the 1976 Educational Equity Act, which authorized the Office of Education to begin preparing "non-sexist curricula and non-discriminatory vocational and career counseling, sports education, and other programs designed to achieve equity for all students regardless of sex."[45]

In 1983, NOW proudly announced that "The last all-male school in the Ivy League became co-educational when Columbia College enrolled women for the first time in its 229-year history."[46] Sex bias in high-stakes testing became an issue in 1986 when NOW president Eleanor Smeal and other civil rights groups organized FairTest, a group that claimed that standardized tests referred twice as often to males and male activities compared to females and female activities. In 1987, FairTest claimed that the sex bias of the SAT and PSAT were denying female students fellowships and scholarships. During this period, NOW investigated charges of sex bias in college hiring and tenure practices.[47]

NOW's long-term hope is, in the words of NOW National Secretary Karen Johnson, "to finally raise sex discrimination to the same level of constitutional scrutiny as race."[48] NOW leaders pinned their hopes on a Supreme Court case challenging the male-only admission policy at the Virginia Military Institute. Although the Supreme Court's final decision left undecided the constitutional issue of race and sex discrimination being equivalent, the judgment did, according to Johnson, affirm that "the qualities important for military leaders—integrity, tenacity and bravery—have nothing to do with a person's sex."[49]

The Virginia Military Institute decision exemplifies the ways in which NOW and other feminist organizations have reshaped educational institutions. In 1996, the report "Opening Doors in Education" detailed the results of Title IX and affirmative action:

1. Female medical school graduates rose from 8.4% of the total medical school graduates in 1969 to 34.5% in 1990.
2. Women increased their share of doctoral and professional degrees from 14.4% of doctorates in 1971 to 36.8% in 1991.

3. Affirmative action and federal legislation increased women's opportunities in vocational education.

4. Female involvement in high school and college athletics increased
with participation in high school athletics increasing from 7% in
1972 of the total number of students in athletics to 37% in 1992 and
in college from 15.6% in 1972 to 34.8% in 1993.[50]

While citing these accomplishments, feminist leaders continued to
worry about entrenched sex discrimination in higher education and vocational training, the disproportionate number of women without tenure or
full professorships in higher education, and remaining barriers in athletics. The report defended the continued use of affirmative action in college admissions by suggesting that the real preferential treatment in college admissions goes to the "children of alumni—not women and
minorities."[51] As proof, the report disclosed that "children of alumni at
Harvard University in 1991 were three times more likely to be accepted
than other prospective students. At Yale, children of alumni are two and
a half times more likely to be admitted."[52]

As part of the strategy to combat the right, Eleanor Smeal, the former
president of NOW, organized the Feminist Majority in 1987 to help elect
feminist candidates to Congress and state and local governments. Warning about the "unprecedented attack by right-wing extremists," the Feminist Majority issued a statement that "by proclaiming ourselves feminists,
we emphasize what it means to stand up for women's rights, equality, and
empowerment."[53] For the Feminist Majority, the significant issues remain
equality for women, reproductive freedom, and increased human services.

By the late 1990s, NOW and the Feminist Majority considered themselves in a powerful struggle against the religious right and Republicans.
The most heated issue was abortion. Although abortion accounted for a
major part of the political divide between feminist organizations and the
right, education and affirmative action remained contentious items.

As I discussed in chapter 1, the religious right is attempting to gain
control of local school boards so that it can censor textbooks and limit
sex education. Textbooks and curricula that portray gender equality in
the home and workplace are an anathema to the religious right. The religious right is opposed to sex education courses that teach about birth
control and abortion. Therefore, the political struggle between feminists
and the religious right over the control of school boards is a conflict over
the social role of women and sexual values.

Calling it the revolt of "angry White males," the religious right, neoconservatives, and New Democrats oppose the positive affirmative-action

policies of the Rainbow Coalition, NOW, the Feminist Majority, and other feminist organizations. Progressives within the Democratic Party claim that affirmative-action policies that do not take into consideration gender and racial balance will perpetuate discrimination. NOW and the Feminist Majority insist that race and gender considerations are a necessary part of affirmative action because conditions of bias against women continue to exist.

Can unity on the left be achieved through resistance to the right, neoconservatives, and New Democrats? Will a stand against changing affirmative-action policies unify progressives or, as Tomasky found, will progressives remain divided within the Democratic Party?

CULTURAL POLITICS

Criticism of European-centered thinking, or *Eurocentrism*, has enriched and divided progressives, and it has intensified the debate about multicultural education. For example, the Green party is Indiocentric[54] in its definition of "ecological wisdom." The 1996 Green platform asserted that ecological wisdom occurs when "human societies must operate with the understanding that we are part of nature, not separate from nature."[55] In a section devoted to Native Americans, the platform stated: "As Greens we feel a special affinity to the respect for community and the earth that many Native peoples have at their roots."[56]

The religious right objects to Indiocentric and environmental education. As I discussed in chapter 1, the religious right believes the earth was created for the benefit of humans and that humans are distinguished from beasts, plants, and the rest of nature by possession of a soul. The intention of God, according to the religious right, is for humans to exploit animals and nature for their own benefit. Early Puritan settlers displayed their disgust with the unwillingness of Indians to exercise control over nature by quoting from the Bible, Psalm 2:8: "Ask of me, and I will give thee, the heathen for thine inheritance, and the uttermost parts of the earth for thy possession."[57]

In contrast, Native American or Indiocentric thought places humans in the "sacred hoop of nature," where they have the same value as birds, deer, flowers, and the rest of nature. Russell Means, founder of the American Indian Movement, gave this interpretation of Eurocentric thinking: "Distilled to its basic terms, European faith—including the new faith in science—equals a belief that man is God. Europe has always sought a Messiah, whether that be the man Jesus Christ or the man Karl Marx or

the man Albert Einstein. American Indians know this to be totally absurd. Humans are the weakest of all creatures."[58]

Besides making themselves gods over the planet, Means argues, European science reduces the physical universe to a linear mathematical
equation. As gods dedicated to science and technology, Europeans feel
justified in ravaging Mother Earth. European science blinds people to the
interconnections of nature. In addition, science contributes to a material-
istic view, and it creates an unquenchable desire to accumulate worldly
goods. Thus, imagining themselves as gods, Europeans use science to
rape, plunder, and rob not only nature but also the rest of the world's
peoples.

Eurocentric thinking, Means insists, assumes that progress and development are good. *Progress,* in European thinking, means increased control of nature and accumulation of wealth. A contrasting idea is defining
progress as increasing human happiness. Development of nature in Eurocentric thought, Means maintains, involves the continuing subjection of
humans and nature to mechanistic control. European thought gains satis-
faction from development. Means stated in these words:

> There is no satisfaction [for them] to be gained in simply observing the
> wonder of a mountain or a lake or a people in being. No, satisfaction is
> measured in terms of gaining material. So the mountains become gravel,
> and the lake becomes coolant for a factory, and the people are rounded
> up for processing through the indoctrination mills Europeans like to call
> schools.[59]

Means's Indiocentric thinking rejects all forms of European political
thought. Means is anti-Christian, anti-capitalist, anti-Marxist, and anti-
anarchist, concluding that "every revolution in European history has
served to reinforce Europe's tendencies and abilities to export destruction
to other peoples, other cultures, and the environment itself. I defy anyone to point out an example where this is not true."[60]

To everyone except the Greens, Indiocentric thinking is obviously
anathema to the entire range of political thinking so far discussed in this
book. Its anti-Christian message appalls the religious right. Neoconservatives and New Democrats are equally disturbed by its dismissal of
European ideals of progress, development, and science. As a Christian
minister and champion of equal rights, Jesse Jackson is disturbed by its
anti-Christian attitudes and its dismissal of a European-based rights doc-
trine. NOW and the Feminist Majority want equal rights for women
within the current framework of society; in contrast, Native American

advocates of women's rights, such as Paula Gunn Allen, look to Native American traditions as the best means of achieving fulfillment as a woman.[61]

For education, Indiocentered thinking requires going beyond simply teaching about Indian cultures and history to presenting students with a perspective that is non-Christian and non-European. Obviously, many citizens would conclude that this approach would increase social and racial tensions. Moreover, as I discussed in chapters 2 and 3, many people want the schools to unify U.S. culture by teaching traditional Anglo-Saxon values. Others might argue that an Indiocentric education would deny students the skills and knowledge to participate in the dominant society and economic system.

Proponents of Indiocentric and Afrocentric education agree that their major concern involves a way of thinking. On the one hand, as Means suggested, a person of European descent can think like an Indian. On the other hand, many Indians think like Europeans. This is the origin of the famous terms *apples* and *Oreos*. An apple is red on the outside but white on the inside, whereas an Oreo is black on the outside and white on the inside. There are Uncle Tomahawks[62] and Uncle Toms.

Molefi Asante, one of the most articulate champions of Afrocentric education, believes many African Americans are Oreos, including prominent African American scholars Cornel West; Henry Louis Gates, Jr.; and bel hooks. For Asante, these three scholars are "Africans who seek to be appointed overseers of the plantation."[63] Asante identifies three separate Black perspectives: African American, African Eurocentric, and Afrocentric. Those classified as African American, Asante described, as so "well-trained in the Eurocentric perspective that they see themselves as copies of Europeans."[64]

African Eurocentrists, including West, Gates, and hooks, Asante maintains, clearly understand that they are not White, and they recognize the destructive power of racism. The African Eurocentrists seek solutions to problems such as racism in the framework of European thought. They reject anything that suggests separatist thought and separatism. Asante contends that African Eurocentrists are similar to individuals such as Diane Ravitch and Arthur Schlesinger, Jr., who advocate teaching European traditions to create cultural unity.

A review of West's ideas helps to clarify Asante's definition of African Eurocentrists. In the introduction to his popular book *Race Matters*, West provides a poignant example of the continued existence of racism. Even though he is a professor at Princeton University who drives an expensive car and likes to dine biweekly at the somewhat pricey Manhattan soul food restaurant Sweetwaters, West constantly faces racism. He describes going to Manhattan after giving class lectures on Plato's Republic and W. E. B. Du Bois's *The Souls of Black Folk* and watching taxis stop for White people while he is forced to spend an hour trying to get one to stop for him.[65]

Enraged as he is by racist incidents, West insists that to establish a new framework, we need to begin with a frank acknowledgment of the basic humanness and Americanness of each of us. And we must acknowledge as a people—*e pluribus unum*—[that if] we go down, we go down together."[66] West dismisses Afrocentric thinking because of "a reluctance to link race to the common good."[67]

West positions his solution to African American economic problems and racial issues between liberal and conservative political thought. He argues that liberals seek structural solutions, such as affirmative action, poverty programs, and welfare. In contrast, conservatives seek behavioral solutions, such as ending crime and drug usage. In the space between these two sets of solutions West calls for a "politics of conversion," in which African American leadership would help "people to believe that there is hope for the future and a meaning to struggle." The conversion process would be an "affirmation of one's worth."[68] This affirmation of self-worth would overcome the nihilism in the African American community that results from "feelings of horrifying meaninglessness, hopelessness, and [most important] lovelessness."[69] It is nihilism, West contends, that results in high crime rates and damaging drug usage among African Americans.

Therefore, the politics of conversion directly confronts conservative criticism of African American behavior and, simultaneously, recognizes the importance of liberal programs to relieve the poverty and suffering in the African American community.

Advocates of Indocentricity and Afrocentricity would criticize West's solution because it does not directly confront the fundamental reason for the continued existence of poverty and racism. The problem is Eurocentric thinking, which values material accumulation, accepts and justifies inequalities of wealth, and justifies the exploitation and domination of non-European and non-White populations by claims of cultural and racial superiority. As Indocentrists might say, European racism and domination will not stop until Europeans stop thinking of themselves as gods who have the right and the god-given tools to rule the world. From this perspective, West's politics of conversion is nothing more than asking African Americans to join American Whites as the gods of the world.

Afrocentricity, Asante states, "is nothing more than what is congruent to the interpretative life of the African person."[70] Defined in this manner,

Afrocentricity is one of many possible perspectives on interpreting the world, including Eurocentric, Indiocentric, and Latino-centered worldviews. The important thing to Asante is that one's perspective is appropriate to one's life experience and historical background. If a Eurocentric outlook is held by African American people, whose historic roots include slavery, segregation, and economic oppression, then these African American people are blind to the reasons for their continued experience of exploitation and domination. Consequently, they are frozen into inaction. Lifting the veil of Eurocentric thinking and replacing it with Afrocentricity, Asante contends, will allow descendants of Africans in the United States to realize a correspondence between their history and their lived experience.

Once congruence is achieved between African Americans' perspectives and their lived experience and history, then they can develop real and meaningful solutions to their own domination, exploitation, and colonization. In this context West's solution of a politics of conversion sounds to the Afrocentric ear like empty words, whereas to the Eurocentric ear the words resonate with feelings of truth and goodness. On the one hand, Eurocentrists can feel comfortable and not endangered, because West's words conform to their vision of the world. On the other hand, because proposals emerging from Afrocentricity do not fit into the history and lived experiences of Europeans, Eurocentrists must labor for an understanding. The foreign sounds of Afrocentric words often seem hostile to Eurocentric ears. In fact, the outright violence of European colonialists in modern African history results in an Afrocentric message containing actual hostility toward Eurocentrism and creates dissonance with Eurocentric intellectual frameworks.

A good example of Eurocentrists feeling threatened is the debate over the contributions of Egypt to the development in ancient Greece of art, mathematics, science, and philosophy. Whereas Europeans have traditionally looked to ancient Greece as the source of their intellectual development, they have neglected an examination of the possible contributions of ancient Egypt to ancient Greece. Egypt, of course, is in Africa. European colonialism and exploitation of Africa were justified by claims that Europeans had the most advanced civilization in the world. What happens to this justification if it can be shown that the roots of European civilization are in Africa?

Eurocentric protests rocked the education world in the late 1980s with the publication of Martin Bernal's *Black Athena* and the distribution of Portland, Oregon's, Baseline curriculum.[71] Both works placed the origins of Greek civilization in ancient Egypt with the assertion that the population of ancient Egypt was Black. Both claimed that racist attitudes blinded traditional European historians to the possible connection.

Also, the debate over the issue of Greece and Egypt is a good example of recentering a person's thinking! Africa and Black Africans as the source of European superiority sounds and feels hostile to Eurocentrics.

Under the heading "HOT TOPICS: June 1996," Diane Ravitch announced to the Educational Excellence Network that the Afrocentric threat to Eurocentrism had ended with the publication of Mary R. Lefkowitz's book *Not Out of Africa: How Afrocentrism Became an Excuse to Teach Myth as History*, and the book *Black Athena Revisited*, edited by Mary R. Lefkowitz and Guy McLean Rogers. "The silence of the experts has now ended," Ravitch proclaimed. She concluded:

> During the past decade, there has been significant interest in Afrocentrism as an ideology and pedagogy in the nation's schools, especially in those with a significant concentration of African American students. The basic theory of Afrocentrism is that ancient Egypt was an African civilization; that Greeks "stole" their knowledge from Egypt; and that racist archeologists obliterated the superiority of Africa as the source of the world's greatest intellectual and scientific achievements.[72]

In writing Afrocentric textbooks for elementary and secondary school students, Asante does emphasize the importance of Egypt in the historic development of science, mathematics, and literature. Asante's two Afrocentric textbooks are *African American History: A Journey of Liberation and Classical Africa*.[73] In *Classical Africa* Asante lays the foundation for an Afrocentric perspective by pointing out that many ancient Egyptians were Black skinned and that ancient Egypt developed geometry to map land boundaries; developed astronomy and a calendar based on the earth's rotations; invented paper, or papyrus; refined architectural theory through the building of pyramids; advanced the techniques of art through wall paintings and sculpture; and, as represented by the Egyptian Book of the Dead, contributed to the world's literature. Asante avoids the issue of ancient Egypt's contribution to Greek civilization. Through comparisons of contemporary photographs of Black Egyptians or Nubian Egyptians with Black Americans, Asante attempts to connect Black American students with their Egyptian heritage. Asante writes: "In Egypt today, the people in Upper Egypt (the south) often refer to African Americans as Nubian Americans. Explain what Nubian American means to Egyptians today."[74]

On the broader issue of the essential historic qualities of an American of African descent, Asante listed the following:

1. Recognizing an irreducible commitment to the project of liberation and freedom. This means that African Americans recognize a different history than that of Europeans. Liberation becomes the project established in the initial enslavement and resistance.

2. Having roots in the great mythic, oral, and literary works of people of African descent.

3. Resonating with the rhythms, textures, and arts of the African world that are the arts produced by the people of the African world.

4. Serving the historical moment on the basis of classical transformations (Middle Passage, Kemet, Congo, Niger Valley, Meroe, Nubia), which may have been forgotten but that exist in the context and content of the current reality.[75]

There is an important distinction between Means's Indocentricity and Asante's Afrocentricity. Means maintains that Native American values are superior to those of Europeans because of their consequences for the quality of human life. This version of the politics of cultural identity seeks to replace Eurocentric values with Indiocentric values. In fact, given the rapid destruction of the earth, some Greens would claim that this is imperative for the continuation of the human race. In contrast, Asante's Afrocentricity is primarily concerned with replacing Eurocentrism with Afrocentrism in the minds of Americans of African descent so that they can free themselves from European domination.

CONCLUSION

For the first time in U.S. history, consumerism became a focus of discussion during a Presidential debate. Will this issue unify progressives? After reviewing the political policies discussed in this chapter, I am struck by the significance of the Green party. The Green party is building a coalition that embraces issues of race, poverty, and gender while stressing the importance of benefiting all people, including White males, by stopping the exploitation and destruction of the earth. Central to this argument is the role of consumerist ideology. At this time, the Green party might be the only hope for sustaining meaningful progressive politics in the United States.

NOTES

1. In recent years there have been a number of books published on the ideology of consumerism. A good introduction can be found in a series of articles published in Juliet Schor and Douglas Holt, eds., *The Consumer Reader* (New York: New Press, 2000).

2. Ralph Nader, "Children and Education." Available: http://votenader.org.

3. Ibid.

4. Ibid.

5. The 1996 Green Platform, "IV. Platform Policy Document: Democracy: B. Political Participation." Available: www.greenparty.org

6. Ibid.

7. Ibid.

8. Ralph Nader, "Why Is the Government Protecting Corporations That Prey on Kids?", 22 September, 1999. Available: http://votenader.org.

9. Ibid.

10. Ralph Nader, "Making Parents Irrelevant," 27 October 1999. Available: http://votenader.org.

11. Nader, "Why Is the Government ... "

12. Ibid.

13. Ibid.

14. Ralph Nader, "Commerce in the Classroom," 12 May 1999. Available: http://votenader.org.

15. Ibid.

16. Ibid.

17. Ralph Nader, "Ralph Nader on Child Poverty." Available: http://votenader.org.

18. Michael Tomasky, *Left for Dead: The Life, Death and Possible Resurrection of Progressive Politics in America* (New York: Free Press, 1996), 11.

19. Ibid., 2.

20. Ibid., 196.

21. Ibid., 198–202.

22. Ibid., 211.

23. Jacob Weisberg, *In Defense of Government: The Fall and Rise of Public Trust* (New York: Scribner's, 1996), 137.

24. See the biographical sketch "Reverend Jesse L. Jackson, Rainbow Founder." Available: www.cais.net/rainbow/, 1.

25. Ibid., 1.

26. Ibid.

27. Ibid.

28. Ibid., 2.

29. The Feminist Majority, "What Is Affirmative Action?" Available: http://www.feminist.org, 2.

30. Ibid., 1–3.

31. Jesse Jackson, "Let Them Eat Grits: Pseudo-Intellect Mixes Race, I.Q. to Justify America's Ethnic Cleansing." Available: http://www.cais.net/rainbow/, 1.

32. Ibid., 2.

33. Ibid.

34. "The National Organization for Women's 1966 Statement of Purpose." Available: http://www.now.org, 3.

35. "Statement of NOW President Patricia Ireland as Hundreds Demonstrate at White House Over Welfare." Available: http://www.now.org, 1.

36. Ibid., 2.

37. "Media Alert: April 14 in San Francisco 500 Progressive Groups Will Unite for the 'Fight the Right' March and Protest March 19, 1996." Available: http://www.now.org, 1.

38. "The National Organization for Women's 1966 Statement of Purpose," 1.

39. Ibid., 1.

40. Ibid., 2.

41. Ibid., 4.

42. Ibid., 5.

43. "NOW Task Force On Education," May 1967. Available: http://www.now.org.

44. "The Feminist Chronicles 1973–1982," www.now.org, 4.

45. Ibid., 14.

46. "The Feminist Chronicles 1983–1992." Available: http://www.now.org, 4.

47. Ibid.

48. "NOW Leaders Call Supreme Court Decision on VMI A 'Mixed Bag' Victory," 26 June 1996. Available: http://www.now.org, 1.

49. Ibid.

50. "Opening Doors in Education." Available: http://www.feminist.org., 1–2.

51. Ibid., 3.

52. Ibid.

53. "Feminist Who." Available: http://www.feminist.org, 1.

54. I find it is simpler to use the term *Indiocentric* as opposed to *Native American* centered. As the founder of the American Indian Movement, Russell Means commented, "You notice I use the term American Indian rather than Native American .... There has been some controversy about such terms, and frankly, at this point I find it absurd. ... All of the above terms are European in origin; the only non-European way ... [is to use] correct tribal names. There is also some confusion about the word Indian, a mistaken belief that it refers somehow to the country India. Europeans were calling that country Hindustan in 1492. Look it up on the old maps. Columbus called the tribal people he met "Indio" from the Italian in dio meaning in God." Russell Means, *Where White Men Fear to Tread: The Autobiography of Russell Means* (New York: St. Martin's, 1995), 545–546.

55. The 1996 Green Party platform, II. Green Values: 3. Ecological Wisdom. Available: www.greenparty.org

56. IV. Platform Policy Document: Social Justice and Equal Opportunity: H. Native Americans.

57. I explore the cultural contrasts between Indians and European settlers in Joel Spring, *The Cultural Transformation of a Native American Family and Its Tribe 1763–1995* (Mahwah, NJ: Lawrence Erlbaum Associates, Inc., 1996), 12–31.

58. Means, *Where White Men Fear to Tread*, 551.

59. Ibid., 548.

60. Ibid.

61. Paula Gunn Allen, *The Sacred Hoop: Recovering the Feminine in American Indian Traditions* (Boston: Beacon, 1992).

62. For a discussion of the origin of terms *Uncle Tomahawks* and *Red Power*, see Alvin M. Josephy, Jr., ed., *The New Indian Patriots," Red Power: The American Indians' Fight for Freedom* (Lincoln: University of Nebraska Press, 1971), 1–15.

63. Molefi Kete Asante, *Malcolm X as Cultural Hero and Other Afrocentric Essays* (Trenton, NJ: Africa World, 1993), 5.

64. Ibid.

65. Cornel West, *Race Matters* (New York: Vintage, 1994), xiii–xvi.

66. Ibid., 8.

67. Ibid.

68. Ibid.

69. Ibid.

70. Asante, *Malcolm X*, 5.

71. As examples of the criticisms of Bernal's Black Athena and the Portland Baseline curriculum see, Erich Martel, " ... And How Not To: A Critique of the Portland Baseline Essays," *American Educator* (spring 1994), and Frank J. Yurco, "How To Teach Ancient History: A Multicultural Model," *American Educator* (spring 1994).

72. Diane Ravitch, "HOT TOPICS June 96: The Last Word on Afrocentrism? Available: http://www.a1.com/hudson.

73. Molefi Kete Asante, *African American History: A Journey of Liberation* (Rochelle Park, NJ: The Peoples Publishing Group, 1996) and *Classical Africa* (Rochelle Park, NJ: The Peoples Publishing Group, 1994).

74. Asante, *Classical Africa*, 25.

75. Asante, *Malcolm X*, 18.

Chapter 6

Putting It Together

◆ ◆ ◆

I fear that national and state academic standards and tests will place a stranglehold on free thought. The immense political influence of the Christian Coalition and conservative think tanks will ensure that the content of these academic standards and tests will hew to a particular ideological line.

At the 1996 History of Education meeting in Toronto, I asked neoconservative Diane Ravitch about the history standards. Stressing the importance of regulating the school curriculum, she answered, "I want the right attitudes developed by history instruction." What are the right attitudes? Who should have the power to determine these attitudes? As Austrian economists argue, the problem is not the existence of a particular ideology but the use of government to enforce that ideology.

As New Democrats and neoconservatives continue their relentless crusade for academic standards and tests to regulate the school curriculum, they are creating a new class of educational experts to design and implement these instruments of control. These educational experts illustrate the symbiotic relationship between intellectuals and government. The test makers and standard writers depend on government support and therefore continue to supply ideological justification for government regulation of the content of schooling.

I admire the efforts of the religious right to create private schools that reflect their religious values, but I am disturbed and angered by their efforts to impose their values on the rest of the population. The problem is that the religious right believes it their moral imperative to aggressively pursue evangelical policies that force all people to act as good Christians. Swept up by religious zeal, they could, along with advocates of standards and tests, make U.S. public schools the instruments of intellectual totalitarianism.

Choice, charter, and for-profit schools are meaningless if there is no intellectual diversity in the curriculum. These reform plans become a new means of achieving the same goal of controlling what students learn. For-profit schools may be the new frontier of a consumer society. Brand names may replace traditional high school symbols on varsity sweaters.

It is reprehensible that the Republican and Democratic parties remain silent on the issue of unequal funding of schools. Without equal funding of schools, academic standards and high-stakes tests will widen the gap between the rich and the poor. The efforts of New Democrats to make credentials and test scores a key feature of the labor market will, without equal school funding, sharpen social class lines. The United States will become a mandarin society, with tight controls over the ideas to which students are exposed in school. The poor will be taught to love the very system of academic standards and tests that condemns them to a life of low-paying and meaningless work.

I reject the idea that the primary purpose of schooling and education should be increasing economic competitiveness and improving workers' skills. I firmly believe that the goal of government and education should be maximization of human happiness. Thinking is pleasure. Schools have removed pleasure from thinking as they turn the human mind into a commodity to be used by global corporations.

What about the politics of culture? I believe the goal of multicultural education should be to explore other cultures for the purpose of evaluating and changing the values of our society. I do not believe that the only purpose is to create cultural tolerance. Coming from a long line of White Indians—Europeans who joined Indian tribes—I believe U.S. society can learn a great deal from Native American values about sharing wealth, about a human's place in nature, and about pleasure.

Only the Green party spoke out against the commercialization of American schools during the 2000 elections. Only the Green party focused on consumer issues as related to children and the consequences of a consumer culture for political activism. Only the Green party raised the issue of environmentalism in the context of consumerist ideology and suggested that children must be protect from the ideology that supports any environmentally destructive economic system. One would think that environmental education would be at the top of most political parties' educational agenda. However, environmental education might threaten corporations and reduce their financing of political campaigns. Unfortunately, environmentalism is political.

I have created Tables 6.1 through 6.4 to compare and summarize the conflicting and overlapping political positions on education. Obviously, the tables cannot portray the complexity of the issues or the origins and strategies of organizations such as the Christian Coalition, conservative think tanks, New Democrats, the Green Party, the Rainbow Coalition, and the National Organization of Women. Understanding the tables requires a reading of the preceding chapters. These tables can serve only as guides.

In reading these tables, readers should keep in mind the following principles.

- There will be some empty cells, because some organizations do not have a position on every educational issue.
- There is overlap between categories.
- There is no readily identifiable organization for Indocentricity and Afrocentricity. Consequently, I simply identify them by their descriptive names. It is interesting that Indocentricity and Afrocentricity have become widely debated although there is no major political organization, except the Green party, that advocates these cultural positions.

TABLE 6.1
Major Educational Concerns and Choice/Charter

Group(s)	Major Educational Concerns	Choice/Charter
Christian Coalition and the religious right	Want (a) a system of private–public choice that will allow existence of Christian schools and (b) removal of secular humanism from the public school curriculum and textbooks and restriction of sex education to teaching about chastity.	Favor public–private choice and charter schools as a means of providing a Christian alternative to parents. Funding would be by voucher or tuition tax credits.
Conservative think tanks	Forming public attitudes and policies to favor the application of free market/Austrian economics to education. Strong opposition to the educational bureaucracy and multicultural education.	Favor public–private choice and charter schools, including for-profit schools, religious schools, private schools, and public schools. Believe a free market for schools will limit the power of the educational bureaucracy.

(Continued)

TABLE 6.1

(Continued)

Group(s)	Major Educational Concerns	Choice/Charter
Neoconservatives	Establishing federal or state academic standards and tests. Want to maintain the moral and social authority of government while the free market manages schools. Consider the major education problems to be the bureaucracy, progressive teaching methods, and multicultural education.	Favor federal and state academic standards to regulate public–private choice and charter schools composed of for-profit schools, religious schools, private schools, and public schools.
2000 Republican platform	Requiring states to administer statewide testing programs, grading of schools, providing vouchers to parents of failing schools so they can choose private or other public schools, and special funds for reading programs.	Federal financing of private–public voucher plan for parents of children in failing schools.
New Democrats	Increasing the educational level of American workers for competition in the world labor market. Reductions in inequalities in wealth will result from improved educational opportunities and improved schools.	Support choice/charter schools within a public school system. Similar to neoconservatives in wanting choice/charter schools to be regulated by federal or state academic standards.
Green party	Commercialization of education; the targeting of children by advertisers; and the exposure of children to violence in movies, video games, and television programming.	In 1996 campaign, favored charter schools and choice plans as a means for increasing ideological diversity in education.
Rainbow Coalition	Maintaining and expanding war-on-poverty education programs and protecting positive affirmative-action programs.	
National Organization of Women	Eliminating gender bias in school curricula, school athletics, textbooks, high-stakes testing, employment opportunities, and college admissions and protecting positive affirmative-action programs.	
Indiocentricity/ Afrocentricity	Developing educational programs that provide non-Eurocentric ways of thinking about the world.	Favors tribal control of schools and vouchers/charter school laws that will allow for the existence of Indiocentric and Afrocentric schools.

TABLE 6.2
Ideological Content and the Role of the Federal Government

Group(s)	Ideological Content	Role of the Federal Government
Christian Coalition and the religious right	Removal from the curriculum and textbooks of all anti-Christian ideas, including secular humanism, values clarification, vegetarianism, environmentalism, feminism, multiculturalism, birth control instruction and abortion, and centering teaching around traditional Christian and Anglo-Saxon values.	Limited to the possible creation of national academic standards and support of vouchers and tuition tax credits for school choice.
Conservative think tanks	School curricula and textbooks should reflect traditional Anglo-Saxon values with an emphasis on the capitalist ideals of Austrian economics. These values are to be the basis of cultural unity.	Limited to the possible creation of national academic standards and support of vouchers and tuition tax credits.
Neoconservatives	Creation of federal or state academic standards that are based on traditional Anglo-Saxon values.	Acting as a moral and social authority by creating academic standards and tests.
2000 Republican platform	Committed to the vision of compassionate conservativism.	Federal government to provide conditions that enhance individuals' efforts to improve their social and economic conditions.
Green party	Opposed to the ideology of consumerism that is responsible for an environmentally destructive economic system.	Control environmental pollution and protect the public from a consumerist ideology.
New Democrats	Creation of national or state academic standards to prepare students for competition in the world labor market. Support teaching tolerance in schools and creating a sense of cooperation as a means of maintaining cultural unity.	Support a federal role in establishing national academic standards; providing lifelong learning opportunities, particularly for the unemployed; maintaining Head Start; and helping more students attend college through tax credits and deductions, loans, and Americorps.
Rainbow Coalition	Elimination of racial and gender bias from school curricula and textbooks, multicultural education, and teaching tolerance.	Providing programs to help students from low-income families gain equal educational opportunity and continuation of positive affirmative-action programs.
National Organization of Women	School curricula and textbooks free of gender and racial bias that provide women with positive role models.	Enforcing Title IX and maintaining positive affirmative-action programs.
Indiocentricity/ Afrocentricity	Educational programs that provide non-Eurocentric ways of thinking about the world.	Allow tribal control of schools for Native Americans. Voucher/charter schools to allow for the existence of Afrocentric education.

TABLE 6.3
Equal Educational Opportunity and Inequalities in Wealth

Group(s)	Equal Educational Opportunity	Inequalities in Wealth
Christian Coalition and the religious right		Inequality in wealth is a natural and necessary result of a free market.
Conservative think tanks	To be created through competition among educational institutions.	Inequality in wealth is a natural and necessary result of a free market.
Neoconservatives	To be created through competition among educational institutions.	Inequality in wealth is a natural and necessary result of a free market.
2000 Republican platform	To be created through competition among educational institutions.	Inequality in wealth is a natural and necessary result of a free market.
New Democrats	Improve preschool education and increase opportunities for more people to attend college.	Improve the educational levels and job skills of Americans so that more can enter the ranks of high-income workers in a global economy.
Green party	Increase taxes on corporations and ensure equality of spending between schools.	Tax the wealthy and redistribute through the rest of the population
Rainbow Coalition	Support preschool and compensatory education programs, increased involvement of parents in schools, and elimination of inequalities in funding among school districts.	Increase educational opportunities, maintaining positive affirmative-action programs, support organized labor, increase taxes on corporations and the wealthy, decrease taxes on low- and middle-income groups, and eliminate corporate welfare.
National Organization for Women	Reduce gender bias in schools and employment.	Increase educational opportunities and maintain positive affirmative-action programs.
Indiocentricity/ Afrocentricity	Tribal control of schools and African American control of schools. Indiocentric and Afrocentric schools will overcome the inequalities resulting from African Americans and Native Americans learning a Eurocentric curriculum.	Help students to understand how Eurocentrism justifies the exploitation of people of color. Provide students with tools to overcome domination and exploitation by a Eurocentric culture.

TABLE 6.4

Multiculturalism and Affirmative Action

Group(s)	Multiculturalism	Affirmative Action
Christian Coalition and the religious right	Favor national unity around a common culture based on Christian Anglo-Saxon values. Oppose multicultural education and bilingual education.	Opposed to positive affirmative-action programs.
Conservative think tanks	Favor national unity around a common culture based on Anglo-Saxon values and the principles of Austrian economics. Oppose multicultural education and bilingual education.	Opposed to positive affirmative-action programs.
Neoconservatives	Favor national unity around a common culture based on Anglo-Saxon values and the principles of Austrian economics. Oppose multicultural education and bilingual education.	Opposed to positive affirmative-action programs.
New Democrats	Favor a multicultural model that stresses tolerance of other races and cultures, and both genders.	Support affirmative-action policies that do not consider gender and race or aim to achieve a particular gender or racial balance.
Rainbow Coalition	Favors a multicultural model that stresses tolerance of other races and cultures and both genders.	Supports positive affirmative action policies that try to achieve gender and racial balances.
National Organization of Women	Favors a multicultural model that stresses tolerance of other races and cultures and both genders.	Supports positive affirmative-action policies that try to achieve gender and racial balances.
Indocentricity/ Afrocentricity	Reflects multiculturalism and tolerance for educational models based on Afrocentricity and Indiocentricity	

Index